I0137156

Marsha & Dale Brethour

The

HEART OF GOD

AN INTIMATE ENGAGEMENT
The Birth of A New Awakening

The Heart Of God

Intimate Engagements
The Birth of A New Awakening

Marsha and Dale Brethour

Ecclesia Publishing

The Heart of God

Copyright © 2020 Marsha and Dale Brethour

All rights reserved. No part of this book may be used or reproduced by any means, graphic, electronic, mechanical, including photocopying, recording, taping, or by any information storage retrieval system without the written permission of the author and/or publisher. except in the case of brief quotations embodied in critical articles and reviews. Published by Ecclesia Publishing, Canada for worldwide distribution

ISBN: 978-1-9995732-5-6 - Paperback
ISBN: 978-1-7772784-4-1 - eBook

Unless otherwise noted, all scriptures are from the New King James Version®. Copyright© 1982 by Thomas Nelson, Inc. Used by permission. All rights reserved.
Scripture quotations marked (AMP) are taken from the Amplified Bible, Copyright © 1954, 1958, 1962, 1964, 1965, 1987 by the Lockman Foundation Used by Permission. (www.Lockman.org).

Scripture quotations marked (MSG) are taken from The Message: The Bible in Contemporary English, copyright©1993, 1994, 1995, 1996, 2000, 2001, 2002. Used by permission of NavPress Publishing Group.
The Passion Translation (TPT) The Passion Translation®.
Copyright © 2017 by Broad Street Publishing® Group, LLC. Used by permission. All rights reserved. The PassionTranslation.com

A Publication of *Ecclesia Publishing*
ecclesiapublishing@gmail.com
www.ecclesiapublishing.com

Copyright © 2020 Marsha and Dale Brethour

www.dalenmarshabrethour.com

Edited, Produced, Published by Ecclesia Publishing

Cover Design by Michael Aviel

Acknowledgements

YHWH, my husband, Dale, Marion Davis & Pastor/Prophet Dwight Allen (CCCOG-USA), S. Elizabeth Gomes (Ecclesia of Burning Ones), Michael Gomes (Freedom City Ministries), Pastors John and Alexiana Tanyan (Partners in Harvest), Pastors Ramesh and Elsie Naraine (Catch The Fire, Scarborough)

Various influences: Pastor James Hackner (FWC-ACOC), Justin Abraham (Company of Burning Hearts), Ian Clayton (Son Of Thunder), Grant and Samantha Mahoney (Moed-Ministries), Stevie McKie (The Dove Company), Jane Schroeder (Fiery Crown and Glory), and various teachings too many to mention, in pursuit of intimacy with God.

Table of Contents

Endorsements

I have known Marsha and Dale since June 2013 and feel so privileged to be called their friend. They are true lovers of Jesus and walk out everything they share in this beautifully written book with great compassion, integrity and humility.

This new devotional is filled with refreshing simplicity and depth of insight. Rather than offering man-made wisdom, there is a sense that Marsha is acting as a scribe for the very thoughts and heart of God.

I found the wisdom contained within both anchoring and grounding. At the same time, it filled me with an expansive sense of God's love creating unlimited potential for me to soar in His purposes.

The scriptural foundations are solid and very illuminating, and the themes of oneness, trust and intimacy emerge with powerful cumulative impact as each entry is read. I highly recommend this book to anyone who is embarking on new beginnings or yearning to go deeper in their walk with Jesus.

~ Jane Schroeder
Prophetic Seer, International Speaker, Writer
www.fierycrownandglory.com

If you are desiring an interactive, daily "devotional with a difference," I highly recommend The Heart Of God by Marsha and Dale Brethour. Their personal encounters in the kingdom of God is a personal invitation for you to enter into your own encounters with Abba.

~ Michael Aviel
Author/Speaker
www.ecclesiaofburningones.com

REFLECTIONS

At the end of each chapter/day, please take a few minutes to reflect and meditate on what you have read.

Find a quiet place, where you can just engage with the heart of the Father. If you like, you can play soft background music, preferably instrumental, so as not to be influenced by the lyrics of the music.

Journal what you sense Father is saying to you.

Author's Notes

I am a lover of YHWH. I am a Son. My heart is to see sons arise, take their place by ruling and reigning from the Father's heart to the world and beyond.

I am not an intellectual, nor am I a theologian. I am simply a woman who loves YHWH with everything in her being. I am humbled that YHWH has chosen me to transcribe these precious words so that our stony hearts will be melted to pursue intimacy with YHWH. Hunger for more of YHWH has always been my motivation. This, in turn, births the longing for the heart of YHWH to a generation. I have learned that the more you pursue YHWH, the more He reveals His nature to you.

There are no words to express my gratitude and love for YHWH. He has breathed life into these words to create an outflow of His love, heart, and nature to a generation of YHWH's lovers. His multifaceted nature is to be held holy and in reverence. His love knows no bounds. Without Him, there is nothing. Some may not agree with the contents of this book. However, I believe Father has allowed me to reveal small aspects of His nature so that we may pursue a deeper relationship with the lover of our souls, YHWH.

I ask that as you read this book, you would view it from the eyes of the Spirit instead of the natural. I would also like to encourage you to go deeper and higher in your walk with YHWH. This book was birthed when Father asked me a question, *"what do you have in your hand?"* And then He said, *"Use what you have."*

Enjoy!

Foreword

If there are three words that could describe Marsha it is, *"Besotted with Jesus."*

Marsha Brethour and I have been friends since the first time we met at the new Catch the Fire Scarborough Campus in the Greater Toronto Area many, many years ago.

When I came into the service, the first thing I heard was a sound; a very powerful sound. I scanned the gathering to locate who was singing so beautifully. And there was Marsha (or Marshee, as I call her)! We quickly became friends and over the years, and we have spent many hours worshiping together.

It is from that place of worship in the secret place and a deep love for Yeshua, that this book, The Heart of God, was birthed. A book about the Heart of God can only be thus called when someone spends time in that place – in the heart of God.

The subtitle really struck me - Intimate Engagements, The Birth of A New Awakening. *"Engagement,"* has an expansive meaning as it connotes a continuous place of encounter in the place of intimacy. This place of intimacy is akin to the *"womb of God,"* and so follows the *"birth"* of a new awakening!

This awakening first began in Marsha (and her husband Dale, co-author and father of my daughter-in-love). The oil of this *"new day realities"* overflowed and spilled right unto the printed page of The Heart of God.

This book is a wonderful mix of encouragements, invitations, meditations, encounters, reflections, awe and wonder! It is also quite transitory as you walk alongside Marsha and Dale in their expanding journey in the mysteries of the Kingdom of our Father.

You are invited to come right before the very throne of YHWH to discover *Whose* you are and who you are. Engage in the daily adventures at the end of each day's *Reflections*, feasting at the table of YHWH.

This literary mouthwatering and tasty meal is Marsha's life, and Dale's. Enjoy the feast!

~ S. Elizabeth Gomes
www.ecclesiaofburningones.com

Day 1
Bringing Honour To The Kingdom Of God

by Marsha Brethour

I keep hearing Father say, *"honour is the key to My kingdom."* Honour is a huge commodity in the heavenly realms.

In God's kingdom, honour is a big deal, and part of being honourable is to put others first. This is done only through the heart of the Father. We must first honour our neighbours before we can bring true honour to God. As we honour and love our neighbours and our enemies, God will be honoured and glorified. There has been dishonour, lack of integrity, and strife for too long in the Body of Christ. We spend so much time tearing each other apart; we lose sight of what God is teaching and showing us in particular seasons in our journey. To be able to identify the seasons, it is vital to walk this journey out with the right motives.

Do you know that you are accountable for not being a true ambassador of God and His kingdom if you get caught in strife? For example, you can deliberately shut others out or sabotage their journey in a specific season in doing the Father's will. You are going against the will of Father, and it can cause hindrances to you later on in your journey and may also cause your brother or sister to lose their way in their journey (Matthew 23:13). You will be accountable to God for this.

Many try to duplicate and even imitate the purposes of others within the Body. This is not right; in that it can only lead to strife and confusion. God has individual calls and assignments for each person within His kingdom. Why then are we striving and competing? It is through the Father's heart of love that we can rise above this snare.

1

We are to recognize that we each have our unique destinies, which has been established from before the beginning of time.

One of God's commandments states that we should love our neighbours as ourselves (Mark 12:31). Your neighbour is your fellow brother or sister in Christ. Why would God give this instruction if it was not to be applied to our own lives? The fruits of the Spirit include love, patience, peace, and joy (Galatians 5:22-23). How do we find love and joy in striving through competition and envy?

We have to be mindful that we do not fall into this trap of competition, which can only cause us to falter in our journey with Abba. There is enough room for all to be a part of what God is doing. Pure motives are imperative; therefore, think about these things. What would happen if we all came into unity with God and with each other? If we are in one accord with God, we will be able to move mountains through His Spirit, which will have a transformational effect in the earthly realm.

If we know our true identity, we are not easily tossed to and fro by this world's system (Ephesians 4:14). We are actually able to rise above to be positioned in a place of true sonship in God and to have victory over our trials and turmoils.

We need to always reflect on Jesus Who is our blueprint, when He was here on earth. What would He do? He loved His neighbours as well as His enemies. I go back to the scripture, Mark 8:36, that says, "what does it profit a man if he gains the world but loses his soul?" Is there gain in self-promotion, striving, and competition? Isn't there more to gain if we walk in humility and love, preferring others above ourselves?

Today, ask God to help you sense the seasons clearly and not be a hindrance to anyone in the Body. Ask Him to help you to love others and prefer them above yourself. Be courageous and upright in everything you do. It is time to fly and soar. Pray for others to be able to do the same so that we can reign in the truth and righteousness of God as real, manifested sons of God.

REFLECTIONS

Day 1

- How can I bring honour to the Kingdom of God?
- Ask Father to show you what this means.
- *"Father, I turn my full attention to your Heart, to your Face. Teach me about honour."*

Day 2
Covered In The Womb Of God

By Marsha Brethour

These last few months, God has been tutoring me in the art of staying in a place of rest amidst adversities. He has been faithful and perfect in all His ways. He has been turning my focus to the details in my journey.

I recently had a dream of myself as a little lamb being carried by a huge lion, which represents Father's presence despite adversities, conflict, and darkness. His presence was so real and intimate that I felt protected and safe. In this dream, God showed me that He has us in the palm of His hand no matter what we may be going through. God loves us so much that He always protects us. I have also concluded that God is good regardless of where we are in our journey.

It has been a humbling and insightful time for me. God has constantly been there with me in such intimacy and closeness during turmoil. He has shown me how blessed I am to be surrounded by friends who display the love and heart of the Father in all they do and say. I am privileged to be a part of a movement of ecclesia who do not compromise and have the heart of the Father towards each other. Father has kept me safe in His arms of protection and love so that I was able to overcome from a place of rest in Him.

Sons of God, we are called to be hidden in the ketubah of God. As kings, we are to advance and move on the winds of the Spirit in a place of rest. I believe God is releasing a new breed of sons who will manifest His glory to all ends of the earth. Our DNA is rooted in the Father. He pulled us out of Himself, and we are intertwined with Him through intimacy and the cross. His blood is alive, and it speaks.

Some may think they have been left behind; however, God is saying that He is positioning you for such a time as this (Esther 4:14). You have been through the refiner's fire, and you have been saying, *"how long must I be in this place?"* God wants you to know that this is your time to arise and shine (Isaiah 60:1-22). The covenant He has with you shall be fulfilled. However, be careful not to miss it because it may not be as you envisioned it, and it will come forth quickly.

God is raising up Josephs, Deborahs, Davids, and Daniels. These are those who will bring forth governmental rulership to all nations. They will be so infused with the fragrance of Abba that every move they make will be groundbreaking. They will be covered under the abode of Abba's heart. I saw scrolls and mantles of strategies being released from heaven to these sons that will be strategic. The traps that have hindered the free flow of God's deliverance in many lives will now be removed, which will create waves of freedom to manifest as never before. Staying in intimacy and rest will cause you to overcome and advance. Engaging with the spirit of Wisdom, Might, and Faith is imperative so that you will be victorious (Isaiah 11:2).

REFLECTIONS

Day 2

- What is my special place in the womb of God?
- Take some time to learn about the *Ketubah.*
- Enjoy the exciting adventure of your Ketubah with Yeshua.
- *"Abba, my heart's desire is to know You and to know where I came from. Here I am (Hineni).*
- *I am surrendering my ways for Yours.*
- *I am letting go of my own mindset and flawed expectations.*
- *I am opening my heart to trust that You know what's best for me.*
- *Cause me to embrace your precepts."*

Day 3
Dispensation Of God's Glory

By Marsha Brethour

I have been so humbled by how much Father loves us as His children. His love overshadows all adversities. I believe God is taking His Bride deeper into His heart. I keep hearing, *"a great dispensation of His glory is coming."* What we see with our natural eyes is not how it is at all. The natural realm is the manifestation of what has already transpired in the heavenlies. This is a new day, and God wants us to trust Him and forget old mindsets. We are to be in unity and not judge others, for we will be judged with the same measure that we judge others (Matthew 7:1-6).

We are already seeing brothers and sisters in Christ fight amongst themselves and buy into the enemy's lies. Evil is being presented as good, and good is being presented as evil. Be careful not to be swayed by every wind of doctrine. Always seek God's face for His wisdom so that He will direct your paths. If God does not birth something, you will not see any fruit. But if it is of God, you will surely see the fruit manifested in due season (Matthew 7:15-21, 6-7).

During a meeting I recently attended, I saw God's angels pouring out gold dust on each person's head. When I asked, *"what does this mean?"* God said, *"I am pouring out a dispensation of my glory upon my sons. No longer will you hold your head down, but I will lift you up. You have all authority as a son, and I have given you the tools to access and see changes in your sphere of influence, in regions and nations. The courts are in session."*

The angelic hosts are awaiting the sons of God to come into agreement with heaven so that there will be a shift and recalibration in the natural. Portals, divine connections, fresh manna, and new frequencies from heaven are being released in this day. *"Suddenlies"* will appear. There has been an acceleration in the heavenlies. I also heard *"the scales of justice have been tipped."* God is weighing our hearts to see if we will move and steward what He has given to us as sons (Proverbs 16:2).

In this meeting, I also saw Abba lighting the Menorah. As He lighted it, each part exploded in brilliance. I said, *"what does this mean?"* He simply said, *"I am the all-consuming fire (Hebrews 12:29). I will consume all that has hindered you and held you back. Trust me. I already paid the price on the cross for you to now walk into who I have said you are."* I believe this word is for all of us in this new day. God is doing wonders in our midst. His love never fails.

He is calling us to breathe His *Rauch Ha Kadosh* (Holy Spirit), upon every situation in our lives. As sons, we have the authority and the capacity to speak life and see it manifested. Our praise and worship are a sweet fragrance to His nostrils. So, arise dear ones, and take your place; move into His newness for you.

REFLECTIONS

Day 3

- *"Cause me to walk in humility and discernment to see through Your eyes.*
- *Cause me to come into agreement with Your original intent from the heavenly realms as a son.*
- *I breathe in Your Rauch Ha Kodesh in worship."*

Day 4
Doors Into Dimensions Of His Heart

By Marsha Brethour

I believe this word is for the Bride of Christ. Let him who has ears to hear, let him hear what the Spirit of the Lord is saying (Revelation 2:7).

During worship, in the spirit, I saw a door that was suspended in mid-air. It was white, and it looked as if it were deeply embedded in the air. I asked Abba, *"what is this all about?"* He said, *"it is called the doorway into dimensions?"* I heard Him say, *"I want you to open it and step in. This is the doorway to My heart."*

When Jesus died on the cross, He became the doorway to the dimensions of God's heart. As we grow in our relationship with Abba, we are invited to go into the mysteries of God's heart. God is wooing us to Him. He is calling us to come up higher and deeper into His heart. As we pursue Him, He will give us the pathways that will lead to waves of His love.

As I entered the doorway that Abba invited me to explore, I was taken into dimensions at an accelerated speed. I saw a dying planet in the galaxies, and Abba said, *"jump into it."* I was perplexed at first, but I was obedient. I jumped into this planet as it exploded, and I was pulled into its waves that pushed me into the very center. Then I heard Abba say, *"speak to it, and it will be re-born and restored."* I did, and immediately I was sucked into it, and with the updraft, I was caught up and then spewed out! I was amazed as I saw the planet became whole again. Abba laughed, *"why are you so amazed? Remember you are my daughter, and you carry My authority."* (John 14:12). I said, *"why are You are showing me this?"* He smiled and said, *"I am preparing you for what is to come. You will have to do these things so that nations will be saved and be re-aligned to my Kingdom of Heaven."* He said, *"keep up, little one. We are going somewhere else."*

He took me to another place that had a veil of fire. I could see watcher angels peering at us through the veil. Abba said, *"Do not mind them. They just want to see what you're going to do as a son."* I saw a fire angel flying over our heads. I felt that God had sent out this Seraph of fire to remind me that He is the all-consuming fire, and He has us covered (Isaiah 6:1-4, 37:16). As Abba kept walking, I could see the entire place transform into a beautiful garden. Father picked up a garden pan and started to water the flowers and plants. Immediately they began to flourish and bear fruit. I heard Him say:

*"My rains of refreshing are coming. Plant my seeds of faith My child, for as they grow, unfulfilled promises will come to full bloom. My harvest is coming, and we need laborers to till the soils of man's heart to pursue their first love once more. Set your eyes on Me. New Inventions and medical discoveries will be coming in this season. You are My beacon of hope to the nations. Forget the familiar and lay hold of the new. The newness of My love will bring forth fresh rain and **raham**. (**raham**: Hebrew word meaning, 'to have compassion and mercy; root for the womb of God). As you draw close to Me, I will draw closer to you. The secret place is your haven."*

Restoration, Refreshing, Reviving, and Release

I kept hearing the words, *"restoration, refreshing, reviving, and release!"* These are the doors that are about to appear, unlocking the hearts of many who have been hidden away. God is saying that He will be restoring all that seemed previously lost. He is also going to revive what was once dead and forgotten. As new life burst forth, God is going to release to the forefront once more what has been locked away.

Abba is calling us to submit our hearts and give Him access and permission to take us deeper into the things of the Spirit. As we live and breathe and have our being in Him, He will work in our lives from the inside out, taking us from glory to glory. We are all on a journey of discovering the many facets of who God is. We should never pursue Him for what we can receive, but instead, pursue Him as the Lover of our souls. Selah!

REFLECTIONS

Day 4

- *"Abba, what are the dimensions of Your heart?"*
- Sit a while, close your eyes and …
- Engage the Door, Yeshua …
- Softly say, *"Yeshua, You are the only Door. I enter into the depths of Your heart.*
- *Let me stand in the door (dalet) of Your heart to be Your door/gateway to the worlds around me.*
- *Let me speak from Life (Chayhei) into the place that needs to be restored."*

Day 5
Engaging the Council Chambers Of God

By Marsha & Dale Brethour

Engaging and Petition for Reformation in the Body

This encounter came out of engaging with Abba in His council chambers. Dale and I went into the courts to petition for our region and the Body of Christ. Our pastor had preached on Jacob's ladder and the angelic beings ascending and descending (Genesis 28:10-22). Lately, God has been dealing with me about the least of these and not leaving anyone behind. I sensed in the spirit that there was something holding back the Body of Christ. I became aware that it was a spirit of weariness that was hindering some from moving forward. We both spoke of this, and we decided to go to the courts with our petition.

Firstly, we repented for coming into agreement with anything that may not be from God. We both presented ourselves as living sacrifices asking God, as our Judge, to search our hearts and for us to discern if there was anything in us. Then God gave me a picture of a wall of bricks. I heard Abba say, *"you are part of my foundation, and you will be strong in Me."* He went on to say, *"I am laying each brick Myself to prepare and mold You into a pillar within My church."* (Ephesians 2:20; Psalm 118:22; Acts 4:11). Our local church has a strong foundation that will bring forth unity and newness in this coming season. (Please note the church also represents individuals as we are the church, not a system nor a building).

Rebuilding the Strong Foundations

Dale then received a download about Nehemiah's mission to rebuild the walls of the city of Jerusalem. Nehemiah commissioned each person to steward and build a particular area of the wall (Nehemiah 2:11- 20). Each person had a sword in one hand and a brick in the other as they built their section of the wall. He counseled them, saying, *"do not despise the day of small beginnings."* (Zechariah 4:10). We prayed into this immediately. Nehemiah had to deal with three men who came to him to sow discouragement and accusation. They represented those who are in authority in regions and who stand in accusation against God and His people of purpose. We both repented and stood in proxy for the church and the regions He showed us. Then we shut the accuser's mouth through the testimony of the words that the Judge (God) released for us to decree. Dale saw an angel step forth with a flaming sword and cut off the tongue of the accusers and take them into dark and slippery places where they cannot find their footing again (Psalm 35:5-6).

As we petition in the courts for our cities and regions, God will give us advancement in the realms of the spirit to have a true sustaining change in the natural.

God's Counsel Chambers - (Scrolls and Verdict for Regions)

Then I was transported to another court setting. I saw twelve ancient prophets who had hair as white as wool, and they were dressed in white robes. They each had scrolls, books, and feather pens in their hands. They were in an in-depth discussion about the situations concerning the world. As they spoke, they started to pass their scrolls to each other until they got to God, who was sitting on His throne. He took these scrolls and stamped them with His seal. Then I saw God take cities into His hands. One city I saw was Toronto and the surrounding areas. Here I saw Him place His hand above the city, and He said, *"I could destroy this city with one stroke of My hand, what will you do?"* He looked at me. Instantly, I felt compelled to ask for His mercy and forgiveness. I fell to my knees and wept as the fear of the Lord overtook me. He then began to show me two dragons that were on either side of these great cities. He said, *"the enemy has taken, stolen and pillaged these cities for too long. As a son, I want you to take it back."*

I stood in proxy, asking forgiveness for not stewarding well what

God has given us. I cried out for mercy, and God said, *"you have done well. Tell my sons that I am weighing their hearts to see if they will stand for their nations and territories in these coming days. I will send new strategies to assist in this battle. Warriors are arising."* He then placed His hand above the city and placed it on a table and said, *"I will place My protection over the city instead, now that you have asked for My mercy, I will give it yet again and again."*

God then took me to the treasure rooms of His heart. Here I saw gemstones that had life, and they spoke to each other. They were multifaceted, beautiful, and full of color. Light frequencies would hit them, and they would be illuminated.

Tree of Life (Abide in the Vine Mandate)

Then I saw what looked like smoke and light. As I looked closely, I saw strings coming together to merge and entwine with each other. It began to grow from a small vine into a tree. It kept growing and growing upward, endlessly beyond the sky. I heard Abba say that it is the Tree of Life and that we are the strings that are entwined into His very DNA to merge into Him (Revelation 22:1-5). He is Eternal and Unending. We are the branches that are to be integrated with Him to become one (John 15:1-11). He said our roots grow deep into His heart.

Dale saw an eagle, and I could hear its cry. He said the eagle represents the prophetic mantle. The eagle stood behind the Judge and flapped its wings. It created winds and whirlwinds. These are the winds of change, winds of refreshing to the sons of the Father, and storm winds against the accuser. Dale further explained that God has called us to stand in proxy for the Body to function as both the prophetic and apostolic.

God reminded me of His word to me when we got married. He said, *"I want the prophetic and the apostolic to be married once again."* These will be restored to function as they were created to be in unity. This will bring forth the government of God within the church Kingdom principles and mandates will bring about a reformation in the church. These decrees have been set, and the counsels of God are weighing the hearts of cities and nations before they can advance. This momentum will continue to bring a new wave of healings and revelations like never seen before. The sounds of forgiveness will pulsate with the very heartbeat of God. This will, in turn, cause darkness to crumble. The Sons of God will arise from the ashes to bring forth light to guide multitudes of people to the fullness of God's Spirit. The baton has been passed to the counselors of God in the council chamber. Judgment has been made, and God has set the tone. New mandates and strategies will appear to give new directions to many.

REFLECTIONS

Day 5

- Today, let us look at some scriptures about the Courts of Heaven – Specifically, the Mobile Courts.
- Here are some scriptures to meditate on:
- Proverbs 25:2; Isaiah 43:26; Psalm 9:4; Psalm 43:1; Zechariah 3:1-10; Daniel 7:26-27.
- Pray –

"I position my heart to partner with the Spirit of Wisdom and Council to petition from a heart of truth and purity. I engage with the angels and saints who are guardians of this region or city to land and legislate the scrolls for this area."

Day 6
Expansion

By Marsha Brethour

I heard the Lord say, *"expansion is coming to the Bride."* There will be an expansion in the realms of the spirit that will bring forth newness of manna to His Bride. Many are wondering what to do in this new era. God will be ramping up His army of angels to invade the evil one's camp.

In a recent heavenly encounter, I saw flying scrolls being released quickly. It landed on people's heads, but they did not seem to be aware that the scrolls were there. I believe God is releasing new assignments and scrolls to His sons. I also think that we need the spirit of discernment to access to receive what is being released. Breakthrough and release are coming quickly. His joy will overtake you, and you will prosper like never before (Nehemiah.8:10 AMP). As you become one with Him in the secret place, He will grant you the desires of your heart (Psalm 37:4 AMP).

God is getting ready to release His glory in a new way. New songs, sounds, and vibrations will take you to a higher level in the spiritual realm. This will cause a shift in the natural realm. Many will and have been crossing paths in the heavenly realms. This helps to connect and create changes that will put into place that which has been out of alignment. A crossing over has begun within the Body. We will see the fruit of this in the coming years. All of creation is mourning and travailing to see the manifest sons activate that which has been out of place in the realms of the spirit (Romans 8:22; Romans 8:19 AMP). As they unite with Father in one spirit, Abba will cause a recalibration to occur in the earthly realms.

I have been taken to various places into the heavenlies over the years, however, God has been increasing up my experiences of going home in the heavenlies in a new way. I am being stretched in ways I could never imagine. The more I grow in the things of the spirit, the more I recognize I know nothing at all. It is in my relationship with Abba and others that I have learned what authentic agape love is. The love of the Father outweighs all my needs and adversities. It is His love that means the most to me (Psalm 136 AMP).

These past days have been just pure bliss in the knowledge of His mercies, which are new and true in all that happens in this world. Without Him, we are nothing. His grace and mercy overwhelm me (Lamentations 3:22-23). I believe God is getting ready to create divine connections with people in our lives. This will create new opportunities to bring forth a great harvest of souls and the fulfillment of scrolls and destinies to many. His love is deeper and wider. He is the all-consuming fire (Hebrews 12:29 AMP), and He is calling us to cultivate relationships with each other. This will cause the fulfillment of love and unity within the Body of Christ. There will be hubs of sons of God arising to rule from a kingdom perspective. Keep in the secret place of His love so that expansion happens in every aspect of your lives.

Our DNA is being changed to look like His. The unknown ones will be conduits to bring forth a fresh revelation to the Bride. Discernment will be released to the Bride in newness to work together with wisdom so that advancement will no longer be hindered. Time is being redeemed. God is bending time to accommodate His beloved Bride. We will see the fruit of this being manifested in many ways. We will see many 'suddenlies' appear and time will slow down in some situations to make adjustments as God sees fit. Angelic activities will increase in the natural. Honour and love will be keys to expansion and enlarging our territories as the Spirit leads (Isaiah. 54:2; 1Chronicles 4:9-11 AMP). Be strong in the Lord and the power of His might and He will direct your paths (Ephesians 6:10-12; Proverbs.3:5-6).

REFLECTIONS

Day 6

- Let us do a simple activation here.
- Let us use two adjoining rooms.
- Now, as you step from one room to the next pray this:
- *"Yeshua, I thank you for Your precious blood. Expand my heart Lord to know You more."*
- Always remember to write what you are sensing or perceiving.

Day 7
Fine Tuning The Seeing Ear

By Marsha & Dale Brethour

Recently, I was engaging with Abba about some events that have been happening in my personal journey. I was taken to an interesting place in the heavenlies. It was called the fine-tuning room. It was very different in appearance, and there are no words to describe it. It was made of pearl, and it looked like a shell or an ear. I asked Abba what I was doing there, and He said, *"I want you to tell My children this*:

*I am fine-tuning the seeing ear in this new season." I am fine-tuning My *seeing ear to pick up new frequencies that will be revealed to My Bride. What seemed to be stolen is being restored. As you incline your ear, you will hear what is coming in advance. I am doing a new thing. There are new sounds, vibrations, and frequencies that are coming that will create new pathways. These pathways will guide your seeing ears into portals that will open dimensions that will cause a shift, which will provide ways of escape and direction to overcome* (2 Samuel 5:23-25 AMP). *I am repositioning, recalibrating, and realigning people's destinies in a new way. I am preparing you for what is coming. These sounds will be heard afar off and will not be hindered or contained. Time will shift and reset as these sounds manifest. When this shift occurs, it will merge and create an atmosphere of true change and unity within the Body. Listen for My heartbeat, for this is the only way to hear this sound. The rhythms of My heartbeat will draw you, realign, and catapult you into a new position in Me. This will also allow for true transformational change and shift within the Bride. Time will be reset and be recalibrated to birth new things of the spirit. There will be no more fragmentation within the Bride. She will be made pure and whole so that she can function as I created her to be from when time began. She will emerge out of striving into a spirit of* *humility, wisdom, strength, and love. I have reassigned new blueprints and scrolls to be released from heaven. Suddenlies will appear within the Body and the earthly realm, and many hidden and unknown things will be revealed. Watch and wait for it. Hold on and be of good courage. All is not lost or forgotten little ones. In My kingdom, little is much. Plant Me in the garden of your hearts so that it may go well with you. Salvations and harvest are upon us, so be alert and not falter. My government will reign upon the just and the unjust. All of heaven is groaning and travailing* (Romans 8:22). *Hearts are mending; sicknesses are being healed; families are restored, and what has been lost is being found. We have entered into a day where what was lost can now be openly found, both in the natural and the invisible realms. We are moving into a day of massive acceleration and supernatural momentum within the Bride. The thirsty and hungry will be filled in abundance* (Matthew 5:6 AMP)."

For the many who have felt as if they have been in unknown territory and unsure about how to navigate this past season, know that God has you right where He wants you. He wants you to trust Him despite what it looks like in the natural. For God alone, my soul waits in silence; from Him comes my salvation (Psalm 62:1, 5 AMP). It is in the quietness of His presence that you are able to overcome adversities. There is an unexpected coming that will be unexplained by man because *"I am doing this,"* says the Lord. *"Do not be weary, for I am with you. I have been weighing the intent of many hearts. I have revealed many of My mysteries; however, there is more coming. I am endless in all My ways, and I will not be contained. Drink deeply of Me and My love so that you will be able to withstand what is coming. Selah."*

*What is the seeing ear? *Chazah* is Hebrew for *the seeing ear and hearing eye.* By definition, this can also mean *the seer's anointing* or *those in tune with God's heartbeat* in the context of this blog.

Note: Hebrew definitions are taken from *Reordering Your Day by Chuck Pierce*

.

REFLECTIONS

Day 7

- Close your eyes and think about His love and goodness.
- Turn the eyes of your heart to Him.
- *Father, fine tune my ear to see you.*
- *I position myself to see what You are saying.*

Day 8
God's Commission In This New Era

By Marsha Brethour

As I sat down to do my devotions this morning, I am amazed at how God speaks to us despite the season we may be in. Many of us face daily storms and challenges within our lives; however, in these difficult, hidden places, God's grace and His hand are very much at work. Our job is to move out of the way with our flesh and allow God to do the amazing in our lives. We will also be able to see His promises fulfilled. God is calling us to be lifted above the storms and overcome from a heavenly perspective. We are called to be above and not beneath (Deuteronomy 28:12-14 AMP).

Last week I experienced just that through yet another heavenly encounter. This experience had me pondering what we as the Body have been called to (Luke 4:18 AMP). Yes, as matured Christians, we know we are called to feed the poor, heal the sick and set the captives free, but are we really grasping what God is asking of us? The key is to do these things daily in our journey through the love of the Father and the cross. God is and will never be complicated. God is always concerned with the hearts of man. It is through the healing of the heart that God flows freely with His love onto the lost, weary and broken. God also reminded me of how important it is to apply the cross to everything we do (Luke 9:22-24 AMP). It was already completed at the cross. We need to believe the truth of what He did on the cross for all (Romans 5:8; 8:34; 2 Corinthians 5:13-15 TPT).

This encounter is not only for me personally because I believe God is commissioning us in this new era in a different and more effective way. I believe this word is for the Body. Let him who has ears hear what the spirit of the Lord is saying.

"Behold, I saw the Lamb of God seated on the throne. He was as a brilliant beam of light that extended across the breadth of the world and the length of the universe; it was a living brilliant light in the shape of the cross" (Ezekiel 1:26-28 AMP).

There was a multitude of angels gathered around His throne; they were bowing before Him in worship. Some of these angels had scrolls in their hands; some had feathered pens and were writing and recording every word that was spoken by God. As I looked, I could see other angels blowing trumpets. As they blew these trumpets, I could see sounds, light, colors, and frequencies that actually caused a shaking in the earth and the galaxies. I also saw the Lion of Judah roaring over nations and regions in the earth. There was much activity going on simultaneously, and it overwhelmed me. I then heard Father say, *"I am sending My warrior angels to unlock the mysteries of My heart to My children yet again."*

I then saw what looked like decrees going forth, and people were being released into their destinies. I heard, *"come up higher and deeper in My love, I have heard your cries, and I have seen how weary you have been. I say this day no longer will you be hindered by brokenness or the snares of the evil one, for this is the time for My promises to be fulfilled to My sons and daughters. No longer will they struggle and be tossed to and fro by every religious doctrines or evil manipulations sent by the evil one. They will rise above and be free to move in what I have called them to do for My glory. Many have said in their hearts, 'this move of God is not of Me,' but I say to you that this is all Me. All of heaven is in unison alongside these heavenly sounds that are being released. Let your hearts not be troubled, for I am with you in every step you make as you take territories in My name. I am giving a new way to you. You have been faithful with little and will be rewarded with much more of Me. What you seek is never-ending, but I will fill you with My love that all will see my glory. You have said you want to remain hidden, but I say to you I have kept you hidden for such a time as this."*

Then I heard the Lord say the words, *"promotions are coming to the Body, My Bride. My Bride has much to do for the advancement of My kingdom. Be on the alert for the kingdom of darkness will increase, but if you stay in your position and set your face like flint, this will cause things to move more into My will for the many I have chosen. Through listening closely, through love, being still, and rest in the midst of the storms, you will be able to overcome. Do not worry or fear what your natural eyes are seeing but keep your eyes fixed on Me."*

God then handed me a huge scroll, which had flames of fire on the tips of each side and edged with gold around it. I took it, and immediately I was taken up into galaxies at an accelerated rate. God spoke, and I could see movements and changes. Then God said, *"you go now and release the decrees of fire that I have given to you. Throw it out."* I did as He asked, and I saw a vortex of a whirlwind appearing that caused mountains to move in the lives of people and bring forth healing and much fruit. He smiled and said, *"you have done well, My child."* He then turned and said, *"remember, I am with you in all you do, so go now and soar, My beloved."*

REFLECTIONS

Day 8

- Today, present or trade any situation in your life for the peace of God.
- Receive His comfort in the midst of uncertainty.
- Ask Him to heal your heart and to remove any instances of fear.

Day 9
God's Got You Covered

By Marsha Brethour

Knight Angels of Protection

On May 25, 2015, I saw a vision of a huge army of knight's angels on horses in full armour on a mountain top. They were lined up in a straight line, poised for battle. I could see smoke coming out of their nostrils. Their swords were drawn, and their shields were in place for battle. I heard Abba say, *"protection is on the way. I've got you covered, be not afraid."* I believe God has a mandate and He has you covered. He has a plan (Psalm 91 TPT).

In-roads, Doors, Gateways and Pathways

On May 27, 2015 I heard,

> *"new inroads are being formed to create new pathways that will cause a repositioning people who are in transitions. I am taking you higher and deeper. Where you thought it was a de-motion, it is actually a promotion from heaven's perspective. I am cleansing your gateways so that there will be no hindrances or the slowing of momentum in the coming days. I am doing a fresh thing. Your view will be made broad and straight. Keep in My presence and I will direct your path. It is in the quietness and stillness that I am at work in your situations* (Psalm 62:1 TPT). *Prepare your hearts for a new rhythm of My glory that will bring heaven to earth. Wait for it! I am not a God Who is far off, but I am at hand. I am mobilizing My army to stand guard to protect those that are positioned strategically on the mountains of your influences. Doors and portals are opening to bring forth fresh manna from heaven. My Davids, Esthers, Daniels, Joshuas and Calebs are being birthed to prepare for the*

fullness of My spirit that will brood over nations in the days ahead. The walls are coming down! The hindrances that have held you back will be demolished. You will experience new freedom in many areas in your life. All the obstacles will be laid to rest. You will see the fruit of your faithfulness in the things of the spirit and of the natural. You will see the fruit of what you have labored for decades, bloom and flourish. Your gardens will flourish and bring forth much fruit. I am creating a canopy of love over you that will never be broken or taken away. Rest and abide in My love."

Keys to a Broader View of Transition

On May 28, 2015, I went to a place in the heavenlies. It was a beautiful house. It was not significant in size to my natural eyes. It looked like a cottage; however, it had stairways that led up into the heavenlies, and it was endless. The interesting thing was that I was on the lower level, but I was not aware of the upper level. It took one of God's sons to show me the upper rooms. I believe God is speaking to us about not staying at the same levels that we have been used to within the spirit. He is saying we need to reach even higher in the realms of the spirit. He is preparing more for us as sons. I believe He is saying we need each other to be united in order for us to move up higher. As we walk in love, honour, and unity, we will see perpetual newness within the earthly realm that will cause His government to manifest, which will bring forth release as never before. Your view and perspective are changing. As sons, we need to occupy what God has given to us, such as our mountains and sphere of influence from a governmental perspective. He has the keys to unlock the doors of our hearts and our understanding that will give us access to a broader view of heaven. These keys are love, joy, unity, hindsight, fine-tuning, pathways, and in-roads in this time of transition.

As I walk with God, I am amazed by His goodness and love for us all. It breaks His heart to see us not honouring and loving one another because His love conquers everything (John 13:34-35; 1 Corinthians 13:7 TPT). We should not allow our souls to rule over our spirit but allow God to cleanse us from all impurities that would hold us back as an ecclesia to function as manifested sons of God. So, friends, be cleansed, covered, and move into what God has predestined for your life. Do not be afraid; God has a plan. Trust Him, and He will direct your path always.

REFLECTIONS

Day 9

- Psalm 91 –

He who dwells in the secret place of the Most High
Shall abide under the shadow of the Almighty.
I will say of the Lord, "He is my refuge and my fortress;
My God, in Him I will trust."

Day 10
Hiddenness In God

By Marsha Brethour

What does hiddenness in God mean? God has hidden the secrets to confuse the 'wise.' In theory, how does this work? God hides us away for many different reasons. While we are hidden, we are being molded for His purpose and plan. He hides us to protect us at times (Psalm 91 TPT). He covers us with His feathers. God is so infinite that we will never know the true depths of why He does what He does when and how He chooses to do it. However, I know that He has a plan, and like the loving Father that He is, He will never let anything destroy us.

God is raising a generation of people that have been hidden, but with a purpose to arise and take their place as sons of God. They love not their lives unto death; they are fearless yet humble. They are full of love and integrity, bringing forth heaven's culture of honour here on earth. They are not about agendas or *'celebratism.'* Their every breath is about pleasing Abba and doing His will only as it is in heaven.

It is in the hidden places that God builds character. We sometimes try so hard to get away from the pain that comes with the molding process that we forget to enjoy the process. God is seeking mature sons who are full of His love and integrity and whose only intent is to manifest the Kingdom of the Father. It is in the time of hiddenness that God is able to prepare and shape you for your destiny. Many of the forefathers of old went through periods of hiddenness. This caused them to move closer to the Father. It is through hiddenness that true humility has its work in us.

For the ones who are hidden, God wants you to know that He is pleased with you. You may think that no one sees you, but God sees you. Remember, God's approval is more important than that of man. Your name is written in the Lamb's book of life. Blessed are the meek, for they will inherit the earth (Matthew 5:5 TPT). God also wants you to know that there will come a time in which He will ask you to come out of your hiding to do His will. Some will go back to hiddenness, while some will be launched into the uncomfortable place of being in the forefront. Everyone has a season. That is why there is enough for all of God's children to shine. The heart of the Father is that we do not fight amongst ourselves, but to live in unity and rest in the knowledge that we all make a difference, and we are all a part of God's divine plan. So, let us cheer each other onwards.

I pray that as mature sons, we will be able to recognize the signs of the times so that the ones that are called to the forefront will not be put down or hindered but be encouraged to advance in unity in the things of the Kingdom. May we be obedient and equipped to come alongside them to support and honour them in Jesus' Name! Selah!

REFLECTIONS

Day 10

- What does it mean to be *meek?*
- Search out the root meaning for this word.
- Wait in silence before the Lord, allowing Him to shine His light in your heart.
- Allow Him to search the motives and intentions for anything that He highlights.
- *"Father, I desire to be motivated by Your heart only. Help me to be satisfied to remain hidden in You."*

Day 11
Invitation To A Season Of Courage

By Marsha Brethour

Invitation to the Wedding Feast

We, as an ecclesia, are entering into new territories we have never been before. Many are not quite sure how to navigate these new grounds. I believe God has given us the tools we need to overcome and be victorious in our journeys. God is wooing us as the Bridegroom woos His Bride. He is preparing His Bride for the ultimate covenant and wedding feast (Matthew 22:1-14; Revelation 19:9; Luke 14:7-14). Father is calling us to dance with Him on the sea of glass in true intimacy (Songs of Solomon 1-2; Revelation 4:6; Isaiah 4:4,5 TPT and AMP). Intimacy is everything to the Father. His heart is yearning for His Bride to engage with heaven to bring forth His glory in a new way. The invitation has been given; will you accept it?

In my journey, God has chastened me so that I will be purged with His fire to be as He created me to be. Yes, it is painful, but it is worth it. Honour, love, and purity of heart are only a few keys. God is unlocking hearts with fresh manna from heaven so that we can become His Bride who is without spot, wrinkle and blemish (Ephesians 5:26-27 AMP).

Giftings Intensified

On this journey with God, we need to trust Him even when we cannot grasp what is going on or what is happening to us so that we will overcome and be victorious. He is calling us to advance deeper into the more of who He is. Giftings that have been dormant will emerge in new intensity. However, God will give you the hindsight and the tools needed to understand and use your giftings in the heavenlies to activate and bring forth His kingdom here on earth.

Over the years, in my journey, God has given me many giftings. There have been times I did not understand what they were and what to do with them; however, God has revealed in His timing what they are and their purposes. I was given a particular gift many years ago, and God has been tutoring me on how to use it in the spiritual realms. It has intensified in the natural, which at times is a bit scary to me, but I am learning not to lean on my own understanding and to trust God's leading (Proverbs 3:5-6 TPT). I have heard a leader in the Body of Christ mention this gifting as he too has been taught to use this gift effectively. I am chewing on what God is doing and teaching me in the night watches. God is teaching me to have more self-control by being still and dying to my rights, to honour and prefer others over myself. These are keys to unlock heaven's treasure chest to hope in each of our journeys.

Engaging the Spirit of Might

I have been engaging with the Spirit of Might lately (Isaiah 11:2; Revelation 1, 3, 4:5, 5:6; Zechariah 4:2,6,10; Romans 8:2 AMP & TPT). And I believe God is asking us to engage with this Spirit so that we can be victorious. This Spirit helps us to be courageous to walk through walls that have hindered us in the past. The waves of His fire will consume all that has held us back into freedom. God chastens whom He loves so that we can advance into fulfilling our scrolls to bring forth His kingdom here on earth (Hebrews 12:6-11; Proverbs 3:12; Job 5:17; Revelation 3:19 AMP).

So be of good courage and walk through the walls into freedom.

REFLECTIONS

Day 11

- Take time to engage and allow YHWH to reveal himself to you within your own journey?
- Allow yourself to be wooed by YHWH in face-to-face interaction in the secret place.
- What and how is He revealing Himself to you through the Spirit of Might?

Day 12
New Creation Era

By Marsha & Dale Brethour

As a new creation in Father's kingdom, we are called to not only have encounters, visions, and experiences of the miraculous but to engage with heaven daily. This is a new era we are walking in. All of heaven is waiting for the sons to engage in order to effect changes in this world and beyond. Time is being redeemed and reset. This will cause restoration and new life to spring forth. As we engage with heaven, we will see quick changes. It is not about protocol and formulas, but our heart's condition with Father.

I have been dealing with my stuff, and I have seen the benefits of doing so. The more you allow Father to deal with your stuff, the more of heaven will open up its secrets and mysteries for you to fulfill your scrolls. As salt and light to this world, we are to display the light of Christ in governments and nations. We are no longer slaves and servants but sons and priests who have the authority (Revelation 1:6 AMP), to do what we see our Father doing in heaven. Our Father is releasing blueprints and scrolls from heaven to unlock new doors.

Banqueting Table

There is an invitation being sent out to the sons of God to drink and eat from the lush and bountiful banqueting table of YHWH. As we partake from His table of fullness, we will then walk out our sonship in a new way. We will see a realignment in various ways in our lives. Joy will be a tool that will help you overcome any hindrances. The love of Father will break forth new compassion over people and nations (Nehemiah 8:10; Psalm 16:11; John 15:10-12 TPT).

This love will break down walls in communities, nations, and regions all across the world. Healing will not only take place in people's hearts; it will also bring forth a new revelation of God's scrolls and blueprints to the sons.

Forerunners

Forerunners, do not be weary or discouraged; YHWH has been preparing you for this all your lives. What has been rejected in the past will be restored and become valuable in the coming days. If you have been passed over time and time again, it is because YHWH is your reward. He will give you a deeper understanding and revelation. You will partner with the Spirit of Wisdom and Favour to bring forth much fruit into the kingdom.

The mountains will bow down and melt like wax at the presence of the Lord (Psalm 97:5 TPT). Sons will gain access to cause mountains to move into their rightful place in creation. Breakthroughs in the medical field will be a byproduct of these mountains being moved. Healing from afflictions and infirmities will come suddenly. Those who have suffered will arise and take up their scrolls to create momentum in the universe.

Jesus's Blood and Cross

The blood and the cross of Jesus are available to us as the cornerstone of our faith. His blood speaks, and all of creation will have to bow. His Kingship is not to be made mundane or insignificant, but it must be reverenced and acknowledged daily. His sacrifice is more than communion and rituals. It is His greatest love gift to mankind. When Cain spilled Abel's blood, it opened a gate of hell and murder into the earth. Jesus came and allowed His blood to be spilled to redeem and remove the curse of death. We now have a new existence within the Spirit of Life, in Christ Jesus. This Spirit of Life will be our greatest treasure. Where our treasure is, there our heart will also be. His Spirit of Life stokes a holy fire of deep desire. It will cause us to pursue this desire, and like the wise men, we will leave the place we have known, to lay our treasures before our King. The cross has changed everything (Hebrews 12:24; Romans 8:2; Matthew 6:21 AMP).

REFLECTIONS

Day 12

- See yourself seated at the banqueting table and feasting with the Father Psalm 23.
- See where you are positioned and embrace yourself as a new creation.

Day 13
Overcoming From A Place Of Rest

By Marsha & Dale Brethour

The Womb of God

As I was in the courts recently, I was petitioning God on various aspects in my own life. I saw the womb of God, and it was beautiful and pure; I felt safe and peaceful there. I could hear His heartbeat in the midst, and as I looked, I could see vines and plants starting to grow. I believe God is protecting and nurturing us in the deep places of His womb, and we will see the fruits flourishing in our journey as we go deeper into His womb through rest and intimacy.

I believe God is asking us to overcome our battles from this place of intimacy and rest in Him. We are to ride the waves and winds of His love. His anointing of oil and honey will flow down from the mountains of grace and joy to cause a global reset. Many are facing adversities in life. However, God wants you to know that you are protected in the womb of His love. Just like a fetus in its mother's womb, He has placed you in His womb of protection. He has already given you the tools you need. I believe God wants us as sons to arise out of the ashes of chaos and strife and dwell in the frequencies and vibrations of His heart.

You may be feeling lost, but that is okay because I believe God is taking us into unknown territories in our journey with Him. The way we functioned in the prophetic and apostolic in the past was great, but God is bringing new frameworks. It may not look like it has in the past. A shift has been happening though some may not be aware of it. I believe that as the Bride, God is challenging us to untether from the things that have kept us bound for many years. I believe that as we are released from bondages, it will free us up to move and go deeper in the Spirit of God like never before.

We will need the blueprints from heaven to move into the dimensions of what God has for us to do. Moses went up the mountain and encountered God in the glory and received blueprints from heaven that became the patent for his generation to move from slavery to the promised land. If we remain tethered to the previous ways of operating, we will find it challenging to embrace and engage with Him in His glory and move with Him into the paths that He is revealing now. It does not mean that we change everything for the sake of change or run off to try every new thing. As we delight ourselves in Him, He will begin to touch the desires in our hearts, bringing alignment with His desires, thus establishing us as manifested sons (Psalm 37:3-4 TPT).

Therefore, what seemed good in the past may not carry the grace nor the anointing anymore and may have to be laid down to embrace the new path He is setting before us. This takes courage and faith (Joshua 1:7 AMP).

God is eagerly awaiting us to awake and arise so that He can show us more of His mysteries. There is a promotion in the spirit that has already started. These promotions will continue for eternity. Some seasons will come and go, but the Word of God will endure from generation to generation throughout eternity. I believe God is going to reveal new technology in educational, medical, and scientific arenas. I believe He has already given insight to specific people into new discoveries, inventions, and strategies that will be needed as we go forward. He has released scrolls of new creativity that will help govern different areas of influence in this world. The world will be looking for guidance from the Body in the days to come. There are things in the kingdom of heaven that are complex, but we need to forge ahead and gain more revelation so that we can comprehend (Isaiah 60: 1-4a AMP).

Functioning from Heaven's Perspective

As I have been going places in the spirit in the night watch, God has been showing me various people He has for me to heal, counsel, and observe. In one of my most recent visits, I saw a young woman with three children. The doctors gave her only twelve months to live. I felt her despair and fear as she cried out to God for His healing. God said, *"What are you going to do about this?"* He gave me a choice as to whether I was willing to take my authority as a son to heal her. I believe what God is saying to us is that we need to take our place as a conduit to heal others as sons. We are responsible for being effective and influential in bringing sustained change to the battles here on earth. (Romans 8:19-21 TPT). These changes need to come from heaven's perspective. We have the capacity to convey the frequency and vibration of the heartbeat of the Father. As we visit the ones in need, we will defy time and space as we know it and allow ourselves to function as the spiritual beings we were created to be. It is here we will be effective without being bound by our earthly bodies and mindsets.

In this visitation, I was instructed to breathe life into this woman and to speak shalom upon her, and as I did this, I believed she was healed from cancer. I have never seen her before, but I trust God; He gave me the privilege to heal her, and I am content with doing His will.

All creation is awaiting the manifested sons to come to maturity so that there is a continuous transformation for the advancement of God's kingdom. A global shift has already begun; therefore, be centered in His presence and His word. Keep moving forward to overcome from a seat of rest.

REFLECTIONS

Day 13

- By faith, see yourself seated on your seat of rest in Christ.
- As you position yourself here, allow yourself to be untethered from the cares of the world.
- Meditate and delight yourself in His truth with the word and worship.

Day 14
Sounds and Vibrations From Heaven

By Marsha Brethour

Many are waiting and are quite perplexed as to their next move in the realms of the spirit. We are living in exciting times of the revealing of the mysteries of God. We should never forget our First Love as we expand and engage in the realms of the spirit. For many years it has been my heart that all will come to know Him in intimacy and that the Bride will arise in all her glory to take her rightful place.

One of the keys for us is discernment and wisdom. The word says that my people die because of lack of knowledge (Hosea 4:6 AMP). True knowledge only comes through relationship with Abba. Relationship with Father is vital so that we can move when, where, and at the time Abba wants us to.

Many face challenges with their health, finances, and family losses, but we must forge ahead in humility and recognize God's rulership and sovereignty. God wants us to move at the sound of His heartbeat. It is no longer about brain action but heart action in His kingdom. This time is special and intense. The angelic realms are being activated in a new way. Many are going into the Courts of Heaven to petition for nations and others in a new way. Yet, we are still dealing with these earthly matters. I say to you, *"do not be anxious for nothing but in everything count it all joy."* (Philippians 4:6 AMP).

In a recent encounter in the Courts with a friend, we were able, through Christ, to deal with some unclean spirits that were plaguing my friend. After engaging in the Courts, my friend said she felt much better both physically and spiritually. She was healed from the inside out. I believe God is calling us to be more pro-active by engaging in the Courts on behalf of others as the Spirit leads.

God is calling us to expand our territories to bring forth His good news to the nations. His harvest is ripe, and He is calling forth His laborers to move strategically to bring forth much fruit. For many years God has given me compassion and a burden for His Body. It hurts Him to see us so divided amongst ourselves and to see us perish because we lack knowledge. Some are blinded by the deception of the evil one and his lies. We are being healed to give us access to move into our rightful place as sons and daughters in God's kingdom. This can only come through inner healing and intimacy with Father. God loves us; however, we have been allowing ourselves to be defeated for far too long. We are warriors, and God wants all to know Him and be elevated into heavenly places.

As I listen to the sounds and frequencies of heaven, I have gained new strength to move forward. My very being vibrates to the rhythms of His heartbeat. What is this sound? It is the very heartbeat of the Father in heaven. It is also quoted in scripture *"My sheep knows My voice"* (John 10:27-28 AMP). The voice of the Lord has a dimensional sound that cannot be put into words (Revelation 1:15 14:2; Ezekiel 43:2 TPT & AMP). This same sound the children of Israel experienced in the wilderness (Exodus 20:19 AMP); however, they could not hear it clearly because they were not in the place of intimacy with Father. It is all a part of the fine-tuning of the seeing ear and hearing eyes. It partners with the Spirit of Wisdom and discernment. Creation is travailing for the sons to manifest what God had mandated for them to release here in the natural realm. Living out of His heart brings forth peace, joy, wisdom, and healing. We are His living oracles being released to the dying world.

As I reflect on my journey with Abba, I am amazed by His beauty and love for us all. I have been practicing being in and out of the heavenlies for many years. I did not have the grid to frame it up. However, through the Holy Spirit and others, too many to name, I have grown in the things of the Spirit. I am humbled by God's love for me each day and the miracle He has performed in my life over the years. I am thankful and honoured to be part of His kingdom and His awesome Bride. Shalom

Note: For more on sounds and frequencies read *Phil Masons book on Quantum Glory.*

REFLECTIONS

Day 14

- *"Father, by faith I step into Your Mobile courts."*
- *"I open my gateway of First Love."*
- Wait to see what He would show you.
- Give to Him any fears or anxieties.
- Ask for His blood to wash those places in your heart.

Day 15
Spatial Bursts Of God's Creativity To Mankind.

By Marsha Brethour

I do not understand most of these heavenly encounters, as I am not scientifically inclined. I have asked Abba, *"why me,"* and He said, *"why not you? Remember, I use the foolish things of this world to confound the wise."* What I am about to describe in these encounters I have experienced in the past two days absolutely boggles my mind. These encounters occurred in a time period when I was swamped in my personal life and was unable to listen to any teachings, readings, or podcasts of any prophetic voices. I do not know why God chose to share this with me. I believe it to be *"the infused revelation from God"*- Ian Clayton. (This was quoted to me by my husband Dale).

Please note during this time, I had no previous knowledge of any of these subjects on translocation, spatial bursts, quantum physics, or scientific aspects of these encounters, except the word of God, which is written in my heart. I believe this is straight from God. I would also like to add I have been experiencing translocation for quite some years. I did not realize or had a name for it. I thought it was normal. I have always felt to keep it to myself because it is one of God's mysteries. However, I believe that now the Book has been opened to reveal certain mysteries of God. *"Thank you, Holy Spirit."*

On Tuesday, July 8, 2014, I was on my way to work via train and subway. I had my iPod on listening to my worship music. I started to ask God some questions like, *"what are you doing in my life Lord? What should I expect in this coming season in my personal journey with You?"* He said a few things to me, then I heard the announcer on the train say, *"Broadview."* I had my eyes closed, so I opened my eyes because it was two stops from my destination. I do not know exactly what happened, but the next thing I heard was *"Yonge station."* I thought this is very strange; I must have fallen asleep and missed my stop. I hurried off the train to take the train in the opposite direction to get to work; I waited, and I was about five minutes late that morning. I thought nothing of it except it kept bothering me. I shook it off and thought maybe I'm exhausted or stressed.

Translocation, Creativity, and Medical Breakthroughs

That night I had the incredible experience in which I believe that I was translocated. I have had God take me into the heavenlies for many years; I have been to the Garden, in the Throne room, the Courts, and nations on many occasions. At times I did not know where or what I was doing. These experiences have been fantastic, and they seemed to come naturally to me. However, this time, it was very different because I have never visited so many locations all in one visitation, and I believe I was in many dimensions at the same time. I also think I traveled through space and time, both present and future. For me to make this statement absolutely blows my mind in the natural.

I was translocated to an area that seemed to be the Middle East. This place looked like a desert. I saw what looked like many people in a marketplace going about their business. I saw a man of European descent, and he obviously recognized me because he started to talk to me about the state of medical research in the world. He was very concerned about the lack of resources and creativity to produce medical cures for various diseases, particularly immunizations and vaccines. He went on to say that based on his research, he thinks that if there were a major outbreak of disease, there would not be enough vaccines to cure or inoculate everyone as there were not enough resources or funding available to prepare the world. He also said that the Red Cross had a lot of influence, and they were key to a revolution of new research. He seemed very anxious, and he looked at me for help. He said that we needed miracles. I then thought to myself, *"why is he asking me? I know nothing about medical science, how can I help?"* Then I heard God say, *"Yes, you do; you know Me. I will bring forth new creativity in this area, and this will, in turn, bring forth hope in the hearts of mankind."*

The man smiled, and then he started to speak, and he gave me pathways and insight into how immunizations and cures are done by researchers that filter out to the medical field. I did not understand anything he was telling me in the natural, and I was struggling with all the information then I heard God chuckle and say, *"I will give you what you need when you need it."* I said, *"okay, I trust You Abba."* I was instantly taken to the heavenlies. I saw myself looking out at galaxies and planets, and God instructed me to put planets into place and to release certain things to various people as directed by Him. I was then taken to a room that looked like a courtroom.

The room was filled with angels. I saw myself sitting at a desk with a feather pen in my hand and a scroll made of parchment paper. I was writing whatever God was telling me to write, and then He said, *"give the scroll to the angels."* I rolled it up and gave it to them, and they immediately took off and started to deposit the scrolls to others in the world. In a split second, I was taken back to the man I was speaking to, and he smiled and said, *"I'm so happy to see you again. There have been great changes since I last saw you; many miracles, healings, and breakthroughs of epic proportions in the medical community."* He went on to give me more insights into medical breakthroughs.

I suddenly had a very sharp pain, which immediately caused me to be hurled back into the natural. I looked around, a bit confused, and I rubbed my neck. I looked over at my clock, and it was 3:17 a.m. I asked Abba to help me remember the details of this heavenly encounter, and I asked Abba to allow me to go back to hear the rest of what the man was saying. He said that He would in time. I felt humbled.

I believe God is bringing forth promotions to His sons and daughters. There is a new generation rising up to take their place to walk in the authority God has given them to do what they see the Father doing in heaven. This will cause the manifestation of signs, wonders, miracles, healings, and creativity as never before. Quantum physics and new technology will revolutionize and impact the medical community through research and the development of new cures and vaccines to aid mankind in ways never seen before. Creativity from God will breathe fresh life into how humanity looks at medicine and technology in the near future. The world is looking to the Church for answers, and God will give us the answers, but we need to believe and trust that He is in this new move. All knowledge and creativity came from God, especially the things our natural minds cannot understand.

Prophetic Word on Creativity in Healing - Wednesday, July 9, 2014

On the way to work the same morning on the train, I saw my friend Robin Dhillon. I shared my translocation experience, and here is the prophetic word He gave me. *"God is, and will give you insight into how to heal people, and He is teaching you how to create in the supernatural realm because it is where we learn how to receive the fullness of God's spirit. Then healings will take place and be manifested in the natural. He said he felt like God was teaching me how to bring forth creativity to healing nations and regions through His spirit. God is showing that you can function and live by creating, seeing, hearing, and doing what He does in the heavenly dimensions. He is teaching you how to function in two realms at the same time. It is nothing that you do or work at, but He has made you for this purpose."* I felt very humbled, and I said, *"God, you are really stretching me in this new season."*

Spatial Burst That Creates Time and Movement

I got off the train, and my head was filled with questions for Abba. I remembered my trip the previous morning, so I asked Abba about it. Here is what He told me. He said, *"I am teaching you how to ride the waves of time travel, not to be constrained by time and space, and to function within frequencies. Time and space can be bent, and this will produce a multi-dimensional living. As a son, you can live in both the natural and supernatural realms. You can function in the middle between time and wavelengths of frequencies, sounds, and light. As you travel on the train at an accelerated pace, this causes light, sound, and frequencies to bend the wavelengths, which then causes simultaneous shifts in the atmosphere, causing time to slow down and speed up. Hence, you entered a spatial burst that caused wavelengths to launch your body into multi-dimensions at the same time. Remember, I created frequencies, atoms, molecules, light, sounds, electrons, wavelengths, and vibrations, which are all connected to creativity in human DNA."* God then said, *"I will give you more to this in time."*

I shared this with my husband, Dale. He was very excited and aware that this was a direct word from God. Dale believes that God was releasing me into a mountain of influence to occupy as a daughter. I carry authority and am being tutored and trained in this mountain to bring influence into the nations, medical and healing areas. God uses me to release sounds and frequencies, and vibrations as I sing and worship. I never realized the effect that my sound has in the atmosphere and dimensions of His creativity.

Note: Quote from *Ian Clayton (SOT)*, Prophetic interpretation from *Robin Dhillon & Dale Brethour*. References to areas in *City of Toronto Canada and the Red Cross Inc.*

REFLECTIONS

Day 15

- Allow YHWH to invite you into encounters
- Open your spirit to engage with what He is showing you.
- Ask him to show how to co-create with Him.

Day 16
Speak Life And Live Love

By Marsha Brethour

As priests and kings, we are called to speak life into the people around us. Many of us struggle with the issue of loving the unlovable both within our families and the world. Yeshua has been reminding me that we should love in spite of what we think and see in the natural. Love never fails (1 Corinthians 13:4-8 TPT). Forgiveness is a gift from Father to us because as we forgive, we too will be forgiven (Matthew 6:14-15 TPT). Jesus paid this price on the cross so that His sons will be the light to this dark world (Matthew 5:14 TPT). When we come from a place of genuine love, we start to look and function as true sons to a desperate world. Most of us seek to be loved; why then are we not giving love to everyone around us? This love I speak of comes straight from our Father's heart to all His children. Father is asking us to love more so that we can have real breakthroughs in our various spheres of influence (John 13:34-35 TPT).

When we love, we are able to speak life to the spirit of man to come alive and function as a son. We were created to be a son and not an orphan; however, we do not treat each other as such (John 14:18-20; Romans 8 TPT). This is one of the reasons why we do not see genuine change in our lives as it should. We are to speak life, calling forth heavenly realities to manifest here on earth. This is key (Romans 4:17 TPT). The sons of God have been given this authority by Father, yet we do not release others from bondage with this precious gift. Walking out this journey will bring freedom to so many of our families, friends, and the world if we are obedient to what the Spirit is saying.

God has a mandate in this new day to bring forth salvation and release, so that many will move forward in fulfilling their scrolls. He is, however, asking us to forgive and love so that we can engage and see the fullness of His glory cover the earth. Engaging with heaven in these assignments will bring breakthroughs and momentum that will bear much fruit. The Spirit of Wisdom, Might, and the Fear of the Lord are keys in this regard (Isaiah 11:2; Revelation 3:1, 4:5, 5:6 AMP). You will see restoration and restitution appear. Promises will be fulfilled in the lives of your loved ones if you listen to Holy Spirit and walk the path Father has set before you.

Alignment and positioning are on the rise. Some have already seen the manifestation of this on a small scale. There will be an increase as we engage with heaven and the ancient pathways. The opening up of new gateways will release new blueprints from heaven, then all of creation will align with heaven and time to be restored to its original state. This will bring forth promises, scrolls, and mandates which will be fulfilled suddenly. The frequency of heaven will resonate in His sons to carry this new wave of breakthroughs to many regions. God's timing will bring perfection and victory into many lives that seem lost and hopeless. Continue to legislate from your seat of rest in Father, for as you wait, you will see His goodness appear quickly. Shalom.

REFLECTIONS

Day 16

- Practice speaking *"life"* in your daily walk.
- Feast upon whatever is good and lovely (Philippians 4:8).
- What you speak will manifest; as a son you carry.

Day 17
The Beauty Of God

By Marsha Brethour

I have been thinking very much about the beauty of God. Yes, the beauty of God is a revelation of the very nature of the King of the universe, the great I AM. We first need to look at the attributes of who God is. Who is God? He is Truth, Justice, Saviour, Deliverer, Healer, Counselor, and the Prince of Peace.

Though we may know God's many attributes, sadly, some do not know the awe and the beauty of who He is. As we pursue Him in our journey, He will reveal more of who He is. Sometimes, the problem is our perspective of who God is may be overshadowed by our past experiences or even what others have told us about Him.

God is calling each of us to pursue and draw close to Him to experience who He is for ourselves. In having a relationship with Him, we are challenged not to stay where we are but to be stretched in our ways of thinking. In this, we are growing, and we are better able to see God as Father and also as the Lover of our souls. Experiencing God for ourselves gives us access to the kingdom and the mysteries of God. What we need to recognize is that God will only take you as far as you want to go in Him. He has given all of us free will to serve and know His beauty. It is God's will that all come to know Him; however, because of who He is, He will never force Himself on you.

Other attributes of God are love, joy, peace, long-suffering, kindness, goodness, faithfulness, and self-control (Galatians 5:22-23 AMP). All the fruits of the spirit will be seen in the natural when we truly come to a place of really surrendering who we are to Him alone. It is in this place that there are no hidden agendas or motives. It is here we will see what Jesus meant when He said, *"blessed are the poor in spirit for theirs is the kingdom of heaven"* (Matthew 5:2-4 AMP). The gifting, signs, and wonders are all great, but we need to get to the place where knowing God for His love and beauty is more important to us than the gifts of God.

Today, so many are in pursuit of ministry for their own agendas instead of pursuing the Minister of their hearts, who is the Lover of their souls. God has been saying this to me for a while now. There is no room for hidden motives as only the pure in heart will see God (Matthew 5:8 AMP). We need to allow the vinedresser to prune the dead branches from our hearts continually. This will enable us to bear fruit to bring His kingdom here on earth (John 15:1-17 AMP). This will mean daily dying to self with no self-promotions nor hidden motives. We need to be engrafted in His heart in humility. It is all about what God wants. It is here that we experience no fear of man or being a people pleaser. This, however, will come with criticism and persecution from those who do not understand the deeper depths of God's heart or His mandates.

The Church has been plagued with this misconception that we have to build large ministries to bring God's glory here on earth. However, in the Bible, we never see Jesus building a temple to fill it with members. We see Him having a gathering of hungry people where He ministers to their hearts in love and as a Teacher. As followers of Jesus, we are called to do as we see what the Father does in heaven. If Jesus did it this way, then I think He is telling us to do the same. It is only through His love that the hearts of men can truly be transformed, which will bring Him glory. Selah.

REFLECTIONS

Day 17

- Drink of His beauty of His attributes within your life.
- Cease going ahead of God in busyness and allow His Spirit to guide you each moment.
- Engage with Love and be Love.
- What is YHWH's love language to you.
- Sit still to behold His beauty.

Day 18
God's Heart And Love

By Marsha Brethour

There was a weekend in November 2014, where I experienced such an awesome time with Abba! As I reflect on God's goodness, I am taken back to where I started, and I am reminded of how gracious our Father in heaven is to all of us. The heart of the Father is that all come to know Him for who He is.

That particular weekend, I believe there was an occurrence in the atmosphere that will cause changes like never before in our families, governments, economy, and churches. God is getting ready to do a new thing within the Body. For the past months or so, my husband and I have been very aware of the changes that have been happening in our lives as well as the lives of our friends and families. Everyone is in a transitional stage of getting ready to birth promises in their lives. I believe this paradigm shift that is happening is to root out the things in our hearts that will hinder us from entering into what Father has planned for us. As the word says, *"what can be shaken will be shaken"* (Hebrews 12:27 AMP).

God has been emphasizing to me the importance of having a pure heart towards others and everything in my own life (Matthew 5:8 AMP). He has also pointed out areas in my own heart that needed to be dealt with in order for me to move further in the things of the Spirit. He has been speaking to me about honouring others above myself. As I walk on my journey each day with the Father, I am constantly reminded of His love for me and for all of humanity.

Recently I had a heavenly encounter with Father during worship. I was utterly undone by the pain in His heart for us when we run away from Him instead of running towards Him. His deepest desire is to commune with us daily. There are so many that run away from Him. In our relationship with Him, we will be able to overcome the circumstances in this world. Father has His arms opened wide to gather His chicks to His bosom (Luke 13:34 AMP).

Shifts in Systems in Coming Days

I found the wisdom contained within both anchoring and grounding. At the same time, it filled me with an expansive sense of God's love creating unlimited potential for me to soar in His purposes. In the coming days, we will see radical changes within the world systems and the church systems. Some years ago, God gave me this word that judgment has to come to His house first before we can judge the world system. God chastens whom He loves (Hebrews 12:6-11 AMP). Many are pursuing this world instead of the Kingdom God. God also warned me that we need to ask for a spirit of discernment to discern both good and evil (Hebrews 5:14).

There are ones who are pursuing the power, signs, and wonders but not the heart of God. Be careful to know what is real and what is not. We must be mindful to ask God what He is doing and saying in every situation.

There are many mysteries for us discover therefore I cheer and honour the sons and daughters who are arising, rooted in the heart of the Father. These are those who will experience signs and wonders, and they will be of God. How will we know the difference? Well, by asking God first. Of course, He will give you instruction to test the spirit behind every situation (1 John 4:1-21 AMP). If it flourishes, it will bear good and plenty of fruit. As the word says, *"by their fruits you will know them"* (Matthew 17:15-20 AMP). God is concerned with the heart motive behind the signs and wonders. Has it become all about the hype and self-promotion of building your own kingdom, or is it about building His kingdom so that others may know that He is alive, and He is wondrous in all His ways? God is concerned with the heart always (1 Samuel 16:7 AMP).

The Body is coming into a new day of reformation, restoration, and renewal like never before. We need always to go back to the Source as we move forward. Being led by the Holy Spirit is the key. Engaging the Spirit of the fear of the Lord is the beginning of wisdom and critical in this day (Proverbs 9:10). My heart is that God's name will be glorified and that no one is hindered from what God has for them.

REFLECTIONS

Day 18

- *"Father, help me to be willing to embrace change. I submit my heart for change to be cultivated within me."*
- By faith, step into and recenter yourself back to the gateway of First Love.
- Engage the Spirit of the Fear of the Lord.

Day 19
The Cry Of The Father's Heart

By Marsha & Dale Brethour

I believe God is looking for a generation of people who are willing to lay it all down for Him. We are in a reformation of the church as we know it. Many are experiencing various trials of the heart. He wants us to love each other the way He loves us. We need to stop fighting amongst ourselves. In all the years of my journey with God, I've seen many things within the Body which have hindered us maturing as sons. Disunity and dishonour are two of the most dangerous snares that have plagued the church. We need to love with the heart of the Father.

Some time ago, I saw Abba weeping for us. When I asked why He was crying, He said, *"it breaks My heart to see My children not moving into what they need to move into because they are distracted by building their own kingdoms."* God's heart is that we love each other.

Identity as a Son

Recently, I was again surprised at how many fellow believers have no clue of their identity about who they were created to be. Knowing your identity comes through really knowing the Father heart of God. God as Father is the key to unlock true rest and hope. When you know that Daddy loves you and you know who you are in Christ, you are better equipped to advance into true intimacy with Abba. It is not about your ideas or motives. It is about what is God's plan and purpose for each situation and for each life. As David faced Goliath, he had to respond to God's plan rather than the doubting voice of his older brother and King Saul (1 Samuel 17 AMP). David's covering was his identity in God. David knew God's ways because he had previously defeated the lion and the bear. These victories help us to face future situations and to walk our identity in God.

Identity in His love

We need to reflect on what Abba is saying in every situation we are faced with. How can we love each other if we don't love the One Who is love? Love is not superficial but a genuine heartfelt expression. It is not selfish or unkind; it does not exalt itself above God in any way (1Corinthians 13:4-13 AMP). Knowing your identity will assist you in overcoming. As an overcomer, we are always to ask Abba, *"what are You doing in this situation? What is it that You are teaching me in this situation? Help me to receive what You are showing me. Help me to forgive quickly so that I will not be slowed down in my journey with You. Help me not to be a hindrance to anyone in what I do or say."*

Revelation

Do not allow the voices, whether internal or external, to override the real truth of what Abba is saying. God will work everything out to bring glory. Anything that is not bringing glory to God goes contrary to what God is saying. There are times when God allows us to go through various trials so that we can move into His wisdom and truth. We were not created to indulge in our soulish ways. Our souls need to align with our spirit under His Spirit. Until we stand in the Father, we will not be able to walk as a true son, the way we should. We would be thrown to and fro by every wind in this world (Ephesians 4:14 AMP).

I have been sensing, and God has been showing me that many are not rending their hearts to Him. They are stealing and prostituting His gifts and mysteries within the Body. He cautions us to be careful about how we treat His gifts and mysteries. God is about the heart. I am frustrated when I see the Body tearing each other apart. Is this bringing glory to God, or is it glorifying self? God is weeping for us to get it right as the Bride and to live out of a place of His heart that only brings forth love, honour, and unity.

The enemy is after your inheritance as a son. His chief objective is to steal, kill, and destroy the human race (John 10:10 AMP). The reason is because he realized that God loved us so much that He made a way of relationship for us through the cross. The enemy, on the other hand, has no inheritance or relationship. He blew it! The same tactics he used with Jesus in the desert is the same one he uses on each of us who is a child of God (Mathew 4 AMP). At the cross of Jesus Christ, we have exchanged the lies of the flesh and the lies of the enemy for the way, the Truth and the Life Who is Christ, and now we are to walk out our journey in deep intimacy with the Father. If we believe the lies, then it causes us to walk in defeat and not as overcomers.

I believe we need to be able to overcome our preconceived ideas and expectations for us to be entirely at rest in the heart of the Father. The various pitfalls that hinder us are envy, spiritual jealousy, hidden motives, deceptions, false humility, critical, judgmental spirit towards others, and lack of compassion. Earlier this year, one of the prophetic words coming forth was not to be judgmental of others, as you will be judged with the same or equal measure (Matthew 7 AMP). Where are we in our hearts really? Are we willing to allow Him to judge our hearts first and lay down everything of who we are for Him? It may hurt, or it may be very difficult, but your true reward comes from Him. In this, there is the eternal bliss of His presence and His love.

If we eat from the tree of the knowledge of good and evil instead of eating from the Tree of Life, we are in danger of living out of place of a religious spirit (Genesis 2:17 AMP). This does not reflect the nature of who God is and goes against all that He desires for His children. Whatever tree you choose to eat from will produce those fruits in your life.

Many years ago, I came to a crossroads in my own journey. Abba asked me this question. *"Are you going to be a people pleaser or God pleaser? Choose which one today."* I choose God; what will you choose?

Note: Revelation on the *tree of knowledge* inspired by our friend Robin Dhillon

REFLECTIONS

Day 19

- *"Father, I untether my heart from distractions."*
- As you pray this, wait and see what *Ruach Ha Kodesh* (Holy Spirit) is saying to you.
- What are some of the distractions that is hindering you?
- *"Father, who am I in You? What is my identity?"*
- Meditate and listen to His voice (John 10:27-28).

Day 20
Realigned

By Marsha Brethour

The eyes of the Father are searching to and fro and weighing the very hearts of men (2 Chronicles 16:9).

God is weighing the hearts of men in this day. As we are being fine-tuned to His heart, we will be able to move into new realms of His spirit. His heart is the vehicle of love through which we are able to see an authentic transformation to others, and this same love can be released to a generation.

Recently, God has been taking me into new dimensions of His glory. He has been teaching me in the night seasons to wait upon Him. He is giving me instructions that bring forth change in both the natural and the heavenly realms. We are not to be the carbon copy of each other but be who we are called to be by God. Although we are all a part of the Body of Christ, we all have specific areas that we are called to. God has been showing me how to take ground in the realms of the spirit that will set the tone in the natural. He has commissioned us in our own journey with Him so that we can cross-pollinate, eventually merging into His heart. This will cause the atmosphere to shift and be positioned in their rightful place. God is realigning us as sons and daughters so that we can retrieve any ground that has been stolen or given up.

New Assignments: Realigning to the Original Position

God is releasing new assignments that will bring forth restitution, restoration, and release. In an encounter I had recently, I was taken to a city where I saw a dragon in front of the gates. God told me to slay this dragon, and I did as I was instructed. When I opened up the belly of this dragon, I found precious gemstones, scrolls, and a spear of brass. God instructed me to take these elements back to their rightful kingdoms, which I did. In doing so, I was amazed to see how God has realigned these kingdoms from what was wrong to what was right. Everything resounded with pure harmony, and everything started to move with purpose and clarity like never before.

I believe God wants us to take the authority He has given to us to reposition things in the natural realm. As manifested sons and daughters, we carry authority, both in the heavenly and earthly realms. We must first know who we are in Christ; then, we will be able to function in what God has ordained us to be. As we humble ourselves, God will promote and lift us even higher and deeper into His heart. We are seeing a bit of this recently; however, my heart's longing is to see it globally. I believe that when we stop indulging our desires, we will become God-minded and be able to walk into what God has predestined for us.

The key is that the longing of our hearts should be to see God's kingdom here on earth and to be followers of Jesus who are willing to die daily. As we come together in love and unity with our eyes focused on and through the cross, then we can truly be in one mind, heart, and spirit. When we are in one accord, I believe we will see the manifestations of the great and mighty wonders we will do for God's kingdom.

REFLECTIONS

Day 20

- Meditate on 2 Chronicles 16:9
- *"Father, what is my position in Your kingdom?"*
- *"How do I legislate in my sphere of influence?"*

Day 21
Fix Our Eyes On Jesus

By Marsha Brethour

I was reflecting on the love of God and His beautiful wonder. When faced with trials and turmoil, we need to trust our Father's love, goodness, and His intentions towards us as His children. He instructs us to come to Him as a child, laying down all our cares and fears to the Creator of the universe. However, sometimes we focus so much on our circumstances that we forget that He is the source to Whom we should run. There are many who are so focused on building their own kingdoms that they become ministry driven and fail to give God the glory.

We are living in a time when even the elect can be fooled (Matthew 24:24 TPT). As sons, we have to keep our eyes always fixed on Jesus so that we are not misled in any way. God is sifting the wheat from the tares (Matthew 13:24-30 TPT). If there is any deception, it will be revealed. Purity of heart is the most important component in God's kingdom, for the pure in heart shall see God. We are called to love furiously as the Father loves, yet we must be wise not to compromise our faith in Jesus Christ, our belief in the blood and the cross. We have all come to salvation through the cross and God's precious blood (Romans 3:24-25 TPT). We are never to forget that His blood speaks a better word (Hebrews 12:24 AMP).

The books of heaven are being opened, and the mysteries of God is being revealed to His sons. We need more discernment from Father so that we can have hindsight in the days ahead. God will grant us wisdom to remain victorious against the evil one in his conspiracy against God and His kingdom. Also, having the scriptures as our plumbline will aid us in being victorious in the face of trials and turmoils.

The Word is a two-edged sword that cuts through all darkness (Hebrews 4:12 AMP). The Word is the inspired breath of God to His children. There is no condemnation through Christ Jesus (Romans 8 TPT). We are in a place where we are being tutored to listen, watch, and wait. We are to seek after what the Spirit of God is saying in everything we do or say. If we are rooted in the Father, we will arise victorious in the authority which God has given to us as sons. Many are looking to man for answers when we need only to look to God alone. It is my heart that the Bride arises in all her glory in purity (Ephesians 5:26-27 AMP). God's love is more than enough to take us through the storms and turmoils of this world in which we live. This world is not our home; it is a temporal state. Our real home is heaven within the heart of God (Philippians 3:20-21; Ephesians 2:6-7 AMP).

So friend, fixed your eyes upon Father and lean not on your own understanding but in all your ways acknowledge Him, and He will direct your path and make it straight (Proverb 3:5-6 TPT).

REFLECTIONS

Day 21

- Today, take the time to reflect on where your focus is.
- *"Father, I turn my eyes, my focus, my attention towards you, I look to you. I bring my heart into alignment with Your Word."*
- Purpose in your heart to release to the Lord all the trials. Give them all to Him.
- Allow Him to heal the effects of trauma.

Day 22
The Four Winds Of God's Spirit

By Marsha & Dale Brethour

I was engaging with Abba in the realms of the spirit on some personal issues. I heard Father say, *"start calling forth the four winds of God* (Ezekiel 37:9; Mark 13:27; Revelation 7:1 AMP). *I want you to start releasing My sounds. Tell My sons to release the winds in regions, nations, and territories. Let My sons know that they have to do this with no hidden motives and agendas. I am calling My children to a new level. Do not look at the things in the past but move into the newness. The four winds, when released, will rock the very foundation of this world."*

God went on to explain to me that this should not be taken lightly. He said that the four winds are to be used as a tool and strategy against adversities. It is to release God's governmental precepts to bring forth justice, truth, righteousness, and love into regions (Psalm 97:2 TPT).

Many years ago, when I was learning to be a son, God introduced me to the four winds. I would see atmospheric shifts, and prayers would be fulfilled quickly. I was told to do it by Abba, and I was obedient. However, I did not really understand what I was doing. I also had the fear of the Lord, so I never released the four winds without being instructed by Father to do so. When Father instructed me to release these winds, I knew it was crucial and essential to whatever was going on.

This time, I asked Father what the four winds were, and He said that the four winds are the foundational spirits that His kingdom is built upon. They are Truth, Justice, Righteousness, and Love (Psalm 89:14, 33:5 TPT). These Spirits are interwoven into the seven Spirits of God, which are the Spirit of the Lord, Wisdom, Understanding,

Counsel, Might, Knowledge, and the Fear of the Lord (Isaiah 11 AMP). These four winds should only be used when led by Father because of the power it wields to realign, redeem, reposition, and reset. It has to come from a pure heart perspective. They are nautical directions in motion that (north, south, east, and west) will cause rapid movement in the spiritual realms. He went on to say that *"as you release these winds, that which has been dead will arise and take flight. The Lion and Lioness are My warriors. These are small keys, but they will open huge doors and gates."*

Dale's Encounter

"A few years ago, I was walking on a hill near where I live. I stopped at a certain place as I sensed my spirit being pulled up over the region where I live. At this point, a powerful wind came and blew in the area that I was standing. Winds of change were coming suddenly. I then saw four enormous gates, each at the four nautical points of north, south, east, and west. I turned to face each gate and saw four large metal-like men (guardians), standing in position at each gate. Out of the west gate, I saw a pride of lions running at a fast pace, and as they came to a stop near me, they began to roar over the land. Out of the east gate, I saw a huge waterfall and river burst forth, and living streams of water began to flow over the land. As the south gates were opened, a gentle breeze of His rest, His joy and peace will come. As the north gate was opened, I sensed a somewhat harsher wind that will blow over the Bride of Christ. This will cause her to awaken and be stirred to come out of where she has slumbered and begin to hear the roar of the Lion and to come into His river of joy and rest and flow."

Dale's encounter lines up and confirms with what I believe God is saying to His Bride about the four winds and for us to be of strong courage like lions and lioness.

Oneness with God and Man

God spoke to me about the Bride being in unity and relationship with each other. Oneness with God and man is imperative. Laying down our lives and motives to honour God and man will bear much fruit.

We will see the fullness of God's Spirit being released. Perfect unison brings new frequencies and sounds that will affect dimensions and governments into righteousness, truth, justice, and love. We are reminded that we need each other as the Bride; we cannot have one without the other. We are indeed a beautiful tapestry all woven together in the heart of the Father.

Cross-pollination is vital to build and strengthen relationships and to advance God's kingdom. We must remain alert to caring for each other (Romans 12:10 AMP) and honouring each other as we wait for the winds of the Spirit to blow. The pursuit of the Father is our priority as He shall direct our paths (Psalm 119:105; Isaiah 45:2; Proverbs 3:5 TPT & AMP).

Note: Permission granted from co-author Dale Brethour

REFLECTIONS

Day 22

- For this day 22, sit quietly before YHWH and dialogue with Him about the four winds.
- Only follow His instructions – (John 5:19-20).
- *"Abba, let me ride of the Wind of Your Spirit. I engage my destiny scroll."*
- Be patient and journal what Abba is sharing with you.
- Allow Father to broaden your perspective with these encounters to pursue Him.

Day 23
The Heart Of Thankfulness

By Marsha Brethour

Hope being Restored

I was awoken by Abba this morning with this scripture: Hope deferred makes the heart sick, but a longing fulfilled is the Tree of life (Proverbs 13:12 AMP). What does this mean? Well, I believe God is speaking about overcoming adversities that may cause one to feel hopeless and defeated. We can overcome this by having a thankful heart (1 Thessalonians 5:18 AMP). As we do this, our longings will manifest in the natural, causing new life and fruit to appear.

The key here is to look at the situation from God's perspective, remembering to focus our eyes on Him and His promises. As we keep our eyes on Him, we will see the situation in a new light. The unseen realm always reflects the truth of God's heart towards us. In contrast, the natural realm is usually full of deception and may reflect the opposite of what God is really saying to us. It is while we overcome that we are molded by God's hand to become mature sons and daughters who know their true identity. Only then can we move into fulfilling our scrolls and our destinies to become engrafted into God's DNA. The Tree of life is God. God is looking for a generation of people who are willing to be restored to their rightful place of being embedded into the very heart of the Father. The true purpose of this convergence with the Tree of life is to function as the hands, feet, and heart of God towards others (Revelation 2:7, 22:14; Genesis 3:22).

Prodigals Returning and Restored

During our time connecting with the ones we love like family, other loved ones, and endless activities, we sometimes forget to be thankful.

And though the world is full of turmoil, I believe God wants us to be thankful in everything.

Recently, while at a family gathering, I was struck by how easy it can be to lose sight of having a grateful heart. Many may have loved ones that are unsaved and going through many trials in their lives, but when we focus on the disappointment and unfulfilled expectations, we cannot see God and all that He has planned that will work for our good. Recently, the Holy Spirit reminded me of this very thing – to be thankful. We sometimes wonder if God has forgotten us as we see the ones we love suffer in various ways. Especially in the area of having loved ones who were once on fire for God, yet something happened, and they walked away from Him.

There are times when you may feel a sense of hopelessness and discouragement. Many have been given promises by God that these loved ones will be restored, and they will return as prodigal sons to the Father (Luke 15:11-32). However, though it may seem as though these promises are not being fulfilled, let us remind ourselves that God is bigger than all of these circumstances. It may sometimes take hitting rock bottom before we can rise from the ashes to overcome victoriously. Whenever we are tempted to complain and focus on all the reasons why it may be a bad situation, instead, let us always look at what we should be thankful for (Philippians 4:6-7 AMP). This will help us to focus more on God's plan to give us hope and victory. The harvest is coming; we have hope in this (Luke 10:2; Matthew 9:37; John 4:35 AMP).

Hardships a Vehicle to Victory

As I was reflecting about all the hardships I have endured over the years in my life's journey, Holy Spirit began to show me how He had His hand on me all along, and it was through the pain and valleys that He had positioned me for such a time as this. In the eyes of the world, I may seem to have failed in many areas. From God's perspective, I am doing well, and I am right on track.

The hard places in my life have taught me to be a better person. I am grateful to God for His faithfulness, grace, and His mercies. What

I have endured has become an anchor for me to have a strong foundation in Him. I can now rejoice and be thankful to Him for these hard places (1 Peter 6:9). The value of going through some valleys in life will cause your faith to be built up, which will later be the vehicle to take you to the promises of God (2 Corinthians 1:20 AMP). So, hold on, do not be discouraged. God has a plan that is bigger than you realize. Rest in His love and know this too will pass. Be an overcomer through thankfulness (Revelation 12:11).

God reminded me of the story of Joseph (Genesis 37-50 AMP). Joseph had been betrayed by his brothers; he was forgotten and lied upon by others. He was imprisoned, yet he rose from the ashes to become a king and the leader of a nation. God does not make mistakes. His goal is that you will be an overcomer to walk into your destiny. When you agree with the lies of this world, you are coming in agreement with defeat and the kingdom of darkness. It is through adversity that we see change, which brings forth compassion and your true identity in Christ Jesus. As God begins to deal with your heart, the truth of who you are will emerge so that you will be able to build others up in the faith.

REFLECTIONS

Day 23

- Begin to focus on the goodness of YHWH.
- *"I enter Your gates with thanksgiving in my heart; I enter Your courts with praise."*
- Reflect and meditate on things you are thankful for.
- Begin to verbalize a thankful heart.
- *"Lord, thank you for…"*

Day 24
The Mysteries Of God

By Marsha Brethour

God's Beauty Bringing His Love and His Kingdom

Here is an account of a three-day encounter with Abba in the heavenly realms. As I sit and write this, I am overcome with the love and the beauty of God. He is the God of the universe Who holds everything in His hands.

There is a release of God's glory that is coming like never before. We have been hearing this from many prophetic voices over the years. However, I believe this is the time we are now experiencing. God has been preparing, washing, healing, and bringing us in newness with Him. This new era will empower and enrich our lives like we have never seen in past generations. This coming generation will be the light-bearer of God's glory (Philippians 2:15; Matthew 5:16), and it shall spring forth to affect the nations and generations to come (Isaiah 60:1).

As believers, we are the Body, and we should burn with the passion of His love to bring others alongside us to bring heaven to the earth. No more church as usual but let us be the hands and the feet of God to bring forth His kingdom here in the earthly realm. (Matthew 6:9-11). This is the beginning of a new chapter in our journey with Abba. He wants us to come higher and deeper in Him because there are more of His mysteries, He wants to show us (1Corinthians 4:1AMP). Will you walk into it?

In my quiet time, the Lord has been impressing on me that now is the time for His harvest and His glory to break forth to the world. These encounters that I had over a three-day period have absolutely shaken me to my core. I am amazed at God's wonder and His Love.

The Chambers of God's Glory (Day 1)

On April 30, 2014, I was on my way to work. I was listening to worship and just soaking in God's presence when I was suddenly taken up in the heavenly realm. I saw what looked like a door (Jesus is the Door (Revelation 3:20 AMP), and I saw Jesus standing there. He opened the door with His left hand and motioned me to enter through this door. I saw a bright light coming from the inside (John 8:12 AMP). This light was so bright it hurt my eyes to look at it. I believe it to be God's glory, and Jesus is that Light. I entered through the doors then a miraculous thing happened. I was absorbed by this light, which I cannot comprehend. Inside there was a tunnel, and I started to move at lightning speed. I saw flashes of light, colors, and sounds in what looked like waves all intertwined.

These waves were in unison and moved very rapidly. I asked Jesus, *"what is this place?"* He answered, *"this is the Chambers of Light, sounds, and frequencies of My Glory. This is where My messages will carry My blueprints, and many are released through My Glory. It will be like never before, wait for it, and it will spring forth like rivers of living waters* (Isaiah 43:19 AMP). *This glory wave affects lives and breaks the chains of bondage that will then bring forth healing and salvation to many. The key is to make sure there is nothing in your hearts that is not from Me* (Matthew 5:8; 1 Timothy 1:5; 1 Peter 1:22). *My angelic hosts have been dispatched with the keys to unlock the many mysteries of Me* (Luke 8:10). *I want you to stay close in intimacy with Me, in the secret place* (Psalm 91:1-2 AMP) *and dwell there. I am bringing forth understanding and knowledge in My Heart in the storerooms of the heavenly realms. Rest in My Love."*

The Harvest: It's Time (Mantles Being Released) (Day 2)

On May 1, 2014, during my time with Abba, I heard in the spirit, *"the harvest is ripe, it's time"* (Revelation 14;15). I was then taken again to the heavenlies, and I saw Jesus with a purple coat (royalty and righteousness; 1 Peter 2:9; Isaiah 61:10; Job 29:14; Psalm 132; 9), in His Hand. He handed it to me and said, *"take it; this is yours. It is*

Your mantle. Within your generations, there will be many to come, for My mantles are being released, you need to receive them in order to carry out My purpose and destiny in your lives. This is My legacy to you, My sons and daughters in the generations to come (Isaiah 49:21-22). *These ones will be able to access My dimensions in a new way. The weight of My Glory will overtake them like never seen before. Watch and wait, you will see this in your lifetime, and you are a part of this chosen generation in this new era."*

As I looked, He then took up another coat; this coat was unique. It was very beautiful. It was interwoven with gold and multicolored silk. Jesus shook the coat, and as He did this, I saw the most amazing thing happening before my eyes with every movement of the coat in His hand. I could see creativity, inventions, healings, destinies, and dreams appear to many people upon the earth. I then asked, *"what does this mean?"* He smiled and said, *"this coat is the mantle of creativity; it will also bring forth healings and purpose to many lives. With this mantle, there will be a release that will bring forth supernatural provision and rest. Stay in My presence and take a hold of it so that when it comes, you will know, and you will be able to overcome. I desire that you stay close to Me so that I may take you higher and deeper in Me. With my presence, you will see healings, and My love will pour forth that will change atmospheres. A new freedom and advancement will arise as you abide in Me, so will I abide in you"* (John.15:4-9; 1 John:2:14). *I will be your guide."*

The Garden of His Sons and Daughters (Day 3)

Jesus then motioned to me and said, *"I have something else to show you."* He took grains in His hand, and He threw them out, and as they landed on the ground, I saw that they began to come to life instantly to grow and bear fruit. I asked Him, *"what does it all mean, Lord?"* He smiled and said, *"this is My children, they will bear much fruit, and they have been prepared, watered, and planted. I have handpicked and selected these for such a time as this. These ones are rooted in My love and My heart, and they will not compromise. I am calling them to arise and bloom; they are My beloved."* As He spoke these words, I suddenly saw everything around us transformed into a beautiful garden filled with flowers with sweet fragrances and fruit trees that would instantly bloom and flower over and over again (Ezekiel 47:12). He smiled and said, *"these will flourish, and they will bear abundant fruit for generations and generations to come"* (Ezekiel 17:8; Joel 2:21-22).

REFLECTIONS

Day 24

- Meditate on Colossians 2:2-3.
- *"Abba, I set my heart to know You, to know Your mysteries. Show me how to come into alignment with my destiny scroll."*
- *"Where am I in the Garden of Your heart?"*
- Always wait when you enquire of the Lord.
- Do not be in a hurry.
- *"How can I make a difference in my sphere of influence?"*

Day 25
A Renewed Mind

By Marsha Brethour

In my journey with Abba each day, I am amazed by how much God has equipped us with the capacity to walk into true freedom. He speaks to us in many different ways; however, sometimes we get distracted by external voices as well as our own voice. Our emotions get in the way, causing us to be sidetracked. I am amazed to hear many in the Body make statements like, *"I don't hear from God clearly"* or *"I don't hear at all."* This is a lie from the enemy. We can all hear but are we able to recognize whether it is God's speaking, the enemy, or ourselves?

I have learned over the years that God uses various ways to speak to us. In my journey with Him, He has used His word, other men and women of God, children, dreams, encounters, nature, and movies. This may sound strange to some, but I believe God can use whatever He chooses to get our attention.

How do you identify when God is speaking to you? One sure key is that He always speaks truth and kindness. There is no condemnation or fear in His approach (Romans 8:1-39). His voice is loving yet firm. If there is any indication of self, this is a sure sign that this may not be God speaking to you. Always search your heart before receiving what is being communicated to you so that you are not misled. The more we nurture our relationship with Father, the more we will know His voice (John 10:27-28 AMP). Intimacy with Father is key to access His heart.

Emotions and Pathways

God has been speaking to me about how our emotions are the gateways to our souls. If not renewed under His blood, our emotions can hinder us in many ways in our journey into dimensions in heaven. Our emotions give us access into the brain's pathways that can see and function in another realm. When our emotions are not renewed, this can cause confusion and cloudy vision in the things of the spirit.

God is renewing our minds so that we can function effectively as sons and daughters (Romans 12:2 AMP). As He renews our minds, all our memories and neurons are activated to think the way He does. In the heavens, there are many rooms. One such room is called the Room of Memories. These memories can hinder us or cause us to move forward. Wrong thinking through emotions of sadness, fear, and disgust can cause us to be paralyzed in our journey.

Think about this carefully: with a renewed mind, we are able to think and see what the Father does. Our perspective will change, and our DNA structure will merge and function the way it was supposed to function. The neurons in the brain can get severed if not used. I believe that there are pathways we have not tapped into as yet because they have been severed due to the lies we have agreed with from the enemy. These pathways are encoded into our DNA structure from the beginning of time. I think that as we allow Father to renew our minds, these pathways will start to connect with truth downloads creating new wavelengths that harmonize with the frequencies of heaven.

Thus, this will assist us in effectively walking out our scrolls and destinies. The capacity of the brain is amazing as it can capture our memories and experiences to form who we are. With God at the helm, we can fulfill what He has created us to be through His love. There are many keys that God has given to us through His word to unlock the doors of our minds and our hearts to be reunited with Him. One of the main keys is joy, which will unlock doors of engagement to the heart of the Father (Nehemiah 8:10 AMP).

Joy

The joy of the Lord is our strength (Nehemiah 8:10; Psalm 28:8). Joy frequencies can build new pathways in the brain that bring forth life with renewal properties aiding us in overcoming. When we are filled with the joy of the Lord, it renews the neurons in our brains that connect with the heart of the Father. The DNA strand is a complex structure in the human body; however, if we are sons, made in the image and likeness of our Father in heaven, we all can function as He does. Joy can override negative thinking and bring forth freedom from diseases and bondages. His kingdom is righteousness, peace, and joy in the Holy Ghost (Romans 14:17 AMP).

Our righteousness is built on the love poured out by Jesus at the cross. Jesus took all our shame and sins upon His shoulders, and now He is seated at the right hand of God as our Advocate in heaven (Romans 8:33-34). The spirit of joy brings much life to all the areas of our bodies. Laughter unlocks the doors of despair and pain to bring forth hope. Without hope, the connectors in the brain start to die. This is why the Bible states that hope deferred makes the heart sick, but a longing fulfilled is a tree of life (Proverbs 13:12 AMP).

Joy brings forth light into darkness. Joy is tangible kingdom medicine, and without it, our hearts can be affected negatively, giving place to sickness and bondages. Whatever you allow into your gateways will corrupt and destroy your DNA structure and may cost you your very life. This causes a downward spiral in your life. You will then experience such negativity that can ruin and rob you of the true person you were created to be. God has given us the tools to overcome and be victorious in our journey.

Therefore, joy is a key to overcoming in the Lord. His joy brings forth love, peace, and unity.

Word from Father

We need to take our authority as a son and run with the revelations He has given to us. I believe that we are in an era where we will see manifestations of God's glory dwelling with His Bride. God is pouring out His glory to overtake the darkness to bring forth new manna and life. I believe that the manifested sons are arising to take their place to function from heaven's perspective resulting in genuine change. We are going to see the fulfillment of God's promises to His people come to past. New dimensions are being unlocked. Signs and wonders will occur in new ways. Deeper revelations are being revealed. Scientific breakthroughs are about to manifest and governmental arenas will burst forth to create change. The oracles of God will burst forth to bring freedom and love like never before within and outside of the church.

These oracles are the ones who have been through the Refiner's fire. They love not their lives unto death (Revelation 12:11). They are lovesick and their hearts long for the Bridegroom to appear to rule and reign in justice and truth. This Bride is pure and spotless as she loves the Father furiously and she will not settle for anything less than the love of the Bridegroom (Ephesians 5:26-27 AMP).

Purity of thought comes through belief (faith) in Father. Our belief system has got to change in the way we approach various situations in our lives, having faith in the Father that He know what's best for us. We are told to come as a child in innocence without preconceived notions or expectations. Come as you are to Him, and He will reveal the secrets of His heart to you.

REFLECTIONS

Day 25

- Prepare to take communion and wait quietly before the Lord. *"Father, I submit my mind to You, and I receive the mind of Christ."*
- Meditate on 1 Corinthians 2:16.
- *"Holy Spirit, please show what it means to have the mind of Christ."*

Day 26
The Seed Of God's Word

By Marsha Brethour

This word is based on the Parable of the Sower by Jesus to His disciples. I was having my devotions when the Holy Spirit gave me this awesome word and encounter. I saw in the spirit God's hand scattering seeds on the ground, and I heard, *"harvest,"* then I saw the seeds transformed into people (His Bride). I got a prophetic word for His Bride, and I released it. However, I felt there was more to this, and out of nowhere, Abba gave me this word to add to that word as my husband and I were leading worship at a conference recently. It is incredible how God uses the simple things to confound the wise. I am constantly humbled to see God's handiwork each day in the workings of the Spirit throughout my journey with Him. God will allow certain experiences to happen that will open our eyes to more of Him. He is absolutely beautiful, lovely, and perfect in all His ways.

Will You Catch the Sound?

As I was worshiping, I saw so much that was happening in the realms of the spirit, but I could not quite understand. I saw light, sounds, and frequencies, and I heard say the Spirit say, *"seed and harvest."* I did not understand until now. I heard God say, *"I have created these things in the heavenlies to be released here on the earth. I am releasing My sounds through my light-bearers in the heavens. Ancient sounds are coming to manifest here on earth. Many are talking about the sounds of heaven, yet they do not know what it means. I am able to create sound and use anyone or anything I chose to release it. These frequencies carry amazing components that unlock dimensions and the hidden mysteries of who I am. Will you catch it? You have only barely scratched the surface of what I am about to do in you and through you, My Bride."*

When God releases frequencies from heaven through light and sounds, it can only be caught by those who have made themselves available and ready to hear what the Spirit is saying. When we catch it, it is then manifested to do what God wants, and it produces fruit.

There are times when some are so busy looking with natural eyes for emotional manifestations of God's power that they miss what God is truly doing in their midst. We are to focus on what is hidden from the natural eyes. God is more concerned with the depths of the heart of man than the outward appearances. God is about moving on people's hearts. Through the heart, there is a true manifestation of change, which manifests in healings and heavenly encounters. God is in love with all of us. Many sometimes misunderstand the movement and momentum of God's creativity through these frequencies, sounds, and light in the realms of the Spirit.

Frequencies, Sound and Light upon Hearts

Here is the parable revealed: When these frequencies of sounds and light are released, say through worship, they are like seeds being thrown out by the Father to His children. Some of these seeds fall on stony ground where it withers and dies, while some may fall on fertile ground and bear fruit. Thirdly, some may fall onto fertile soil, but it then gets stifled by thorns and weeds, and then it too may or may not die (Matthew 13:3-14). I had often wondered what Jesus meant when He gave this parable to the disciples.

Seeds upon Hearts that Brings True Harvest

This is the revelation I got from Abba concerning seeds in my encounter. These frequencies (seeds) are thrown out in meetings, church, home, work, and play for us to catch them. Sometimes we do catch them when our hearts are fertile in expectation and humility. This will cause a change within the heart that will then manifest itself in the natural. This may bring forth the fruit of God's glory and Kingdom over time, i.e., healings, signs, wonders, gifting and sonship, maturity. We can call it *"authentic living out of the Father heart of God."*

The stony ground seed withers and dies because there is a lack of expectation, or one may be bound with religious mindsets, ungodly perceptions, unresolved situations, and open doors that hinder the flow of God. Hence, there is no fruit or spiritual growth.

Lastly, let us look at the seeds thrown to fertile ground where thorns and weeds try to stifle it. These seeds are the ones who have heard and are moving in, or towards the things of God. However, the enemy, which represents the thorns, tries to steal its life. The weeds are unforgiveness, ungodly thought patterns, shame, lies, and slime from others through offense and generational issues. These are used by the evil one to rob them of their true destiny and identity in God, which may slow or even hinder advancement in the Kingdom.

The Vine Dresser (God) is willing to prune and get rid of the thorns and the weeds in our lives so we can walk in our true identity as sons and daughters in Him. When we live out of the place of God's heart, we are on the path to knowing who we are and how much He truly loves us. We will then be able to overcome the hindrances through healing and restoration. That will cause us to bear fruit and bring forth the frequencies of His sounds from heaven that will change atmospheres, hearts, and lives. This will be the real harvest for the Bride in this new era.

REFLECTIONS

Day 26

Today, let us do an activation –

- Close your eyes and imagine you are resting your ear close to the Father's chest.
- *"Father, I want to hear Your heartbeat. Align me with the sound of Your Voice."*
  What kind of soil is the seed of the Word being planted?
- What are some things that may hinder the seed of the Word from flourishing?

Day 27
The Tributaries Of God's Heart

By Marsha Brethour

God recently gave me this beautiful illustration of a tree. God is the tree of life that will never die. We, as Christ's Body, are the branches on which God has planted His love. As we move into His heart, we are then merged with His DNA and the strong roots within the depths of His heart, and we will produce much fruit (Psalm 1:3). As we grow in Him, we will remain grounded and rooted, and we cannot be shaken (Psalm 92:12 AMP).

This happens only if we remain in Him by abiding (John 15:4 AMP), for in Him, we live and move and have our being (Acts 17:28 AMP). As these roots grow and spread out into various dimensions, an expansion of tributaries will form to cause a spatial burst of His glory to manifest. These tributaries will reflect His love, grace, joy, patience, and righteousness, causing the very atmosphere to align with His will. I heard Abba say, *"irrigate your roots that they may flourish well."* To irrigate is to water, which means that God is commissioning us to dig deep into the sod of His word.

This sod will train us into a new way of thinking. The old mindset will cause us to dry up and not bear the fruit of God's glory in the way He wants us to. In the sod, we will find the key to unlock the doors of our hearts that will then effect transformational change. God is preparing His Bride for a dress rehearsal to the banquet He has prepared. In order to attend and be present, we need to be correctly irrigated and rooted so that we can move rapidly into the things of the Spirit and not be overtaken. With our roots being firmly planted into His heart, we will not be shaken by any winds or storms that may blow our way.

Faith and courage at this time are crucial. Why? With the faith and the authority He has given to us as sons and daughters, we can petition the Courts of Heaven to receive the mandate to call forth creativity, justice, and unity as God wanted it to be from the beginning of time. The spoken word brings forth creative life (Ezekiel 37:3-5): *"Can these dry bones live? Speak to them they shall come to life, says the Lord of hosts."* God's sod breathes life into our DNA to activate and accelerate destinies of the manifested sons of God in agreement with heaven.

So, speak His life into the areas of your life that may seem dead, so it may come to life, whether it is lost dreams or loved ones, speak life, and your dreams will come to life once more (Romans 4:17 AMP). We were born as creative beings, so begin to move to irrigate your inner man with the sod from His word so that you may flourish and expand to reach nations for His kingdom. Selah.

Irrigate: One reference for the word irrigate is found in the Greek word *"Potizo,"* which means to drink and to be saturated. One usage of this word is found in 1 Corinthians 12:13 AMP).

Sod: The Hebrew means mysterious level or the hidden secret or the mystic meaning of the text (Word of God). In other words, the hidden mysteries of God's word being revealed (Deuteronomy 29:29; Proverbs 25:2; Ephesians 3:9-10 AMP)

REFLECTIONS

Day 27

- Meditate on John 7:38.
- Reflect on the dead areas of your life.
- Ask YHWH to breathe new life into these areas.
- Embrace the restoration and fruitfulness to be infused by Him.

Day 28
The Voice Of God's Heart

By Marsha Brethour

Reflections of God's Goodness and Love

Recently I have been thinking about various aspects of my journey with Father, and I am amazed at how much He has done for me. As I reflected on these things, I am overwhelmed with the goodness and love He has bestowed on me. It has never been an easy road to travel, but God's grace is sufficient, and His love has always helped me to overcome.

God has been speaking to me about the ones who may be overwhelmed and unsure which way to go. I believe God wants you to know that His grace is sufficient, and His mercies are new every morning (2 Corinthians 12:9; Lamentations 3:22-23). He is also saying that He will give you what you need when you need it.

We are sometimes overwhelmed by the many voices we hear, but God knows your heart's desire. He knows the longings of your heart to be in right standing and position in Him. Many prophetic and apostolic voices are on the rise. There will be many teachings, strategies, and wise counsel in this era. But God wants you to know that it is not about the acquisition of information, it is about your journey with Him.

Hearing and seeing in the realms of the spirit will bring forth clarity and confirmation of what God is already speaking to you. God also wants us to listen to His heartbeat and be able to discern the various spirits (1 John 4:1-21; Matthew 24:24 AMP). We are in a crucial time where we cannot afford to be deceived by seducing spirits. We must engage our entire being in knowing the Voice of God.

Stand as manifested sons of God

God is calling us to recognize who we are in Him. Our identity has been under attack for many generations; however, God is raising up a remnant who will know who they are and will give Godly counsel to others to assist them to gain momentum in the realms of the spirit and in their own journey.

God is restoring what has been stolen in order for us to be able to stand on the mountains of influences that He has positioned us to rule and reign as manifested sons so that we are then able to impact the world and bring transformation. God designed man to be a son to have rulership both upon the earth and the heavenly realms. We have been chosen to be the head and not the tail; to be above and not beneath because we are in Him (Deuteronomy 28:13 AMP).

It is in humility that we can truly access the inheritance God has predestined for us. My own journey has taught me that the lower you go in humility, the more He will lift you up. Man's accolades have no meaning; it is only God's applause that we should always seek. Our heart's desire is to see every person come into the realization of how vast God's love is for us and to have true relationship with Him. It is in our relationship with Him that we can know His heart.

From before the beginning of time, God's heart has always been that we have intimacy with Him, and He is calling us to go even deeper into the wonderful riches of His heart. Through intimacy with God, all of creation will be positioned and aligned the way it was supposed to be. God made us for His good pleasure (Psalm 149:4; Philippians 2:3). Think about that for a minute. It is not for His gain but just because He takes pleasure in you. You bring joy to Father's heart every time you take a breath. God wants us to come to Him and partner with Him to live in love, unity, and maturity as manifested sons. God always has our very best interest at heart, even in the midst of pain. He is always cheering us on, and He believes we can and will overcome (John 16:33 AMP).

God wants you to be encouraged, no matter what it may look like in the natural. He says, *"hold on, I am with you, and nothing will harm you. I have a plan to prosper you to bring forth those promises to you* (Jeremiah 29:11-14 AMP). *What I said I will do. I will complete it* (Philippians 1:6 AMP). *Draw closer to My heart in the secret place, for as you seek Me, you will find rest."*

These days will bring forth fruit of salvations, healings, and restorations. The Bride will be in her most incredible days in this coming season. Her attributes will reflect the Bridegroom in every sense of the word.

REFLECTIONS

Day 28

- Meditate on scripture Matthew 6:33.
- Present your emotions to YHWH.
- *"Yeshua, I ask for clarity; I ask to be tutored by the Spirit of Might."*
- Step into the realm of faith and wait for YHWH's guidance.

Day 29
The Vortex Of God's Love

By Marsha & Dale Brethour

Kingdom Shifts and Unity

This week, as God continues to tutor me (Marsha) in the night seasons, I had an incredible dream encounter that has left me completely wrecked with the magnitude of God's love for us. God gave me a word that He is about to change the generational timeline of many who have been faithful in the small matters. I was wondering what this meant when He took me into an encounter where I saw various individuals being transformed by one touch of Abba's hand.

I kept hearing God say, *"this wave of awakening that is coming within the Body of Christ will bring forth an enormous harvest of souls."* It will need a great multitude of laborers in the Kingdom to sustain it. We each must play our part in facilitating the edification of those souls who are being born into the Kingdom of Life and Light.

As I walk each day with Abba, I am more and more aware that I know absolutely nothing. God is pleased with our childlikeness, and He loves when we draw close to Him in the daily routine of life (Matthew 19:14; Matthew 18:2-4 TPT). God is searching and weighing the hearts of men to see who will be approved to take the baton to run into the deeper treasures of who He is.

As you take hold of who He is, you can better understand who you are in Him. His love outweighs your needs, trials, and mistakes. There is much to do within the Kingdom. No more will we be divided by strife and discord, but instead, we will be in one mind, spirit, and heart so that we can gain victory over the evil of this world (Philippians 2:2; Acts 2:1 AMP).

Vortex of His Love

His vortex of love is a place where we need to rest and trust Him to go before us to align and order our steps according to His will. His love will never fail, nor will it ever die (Psalm 136:2; 1 Corinthians 13:4-8 TPT & AMP). It is through His love that His glory and light will forever be a witness to the lost souls in this world. God is about to do some amazing things within the church. There is a new wave of His love coming upon His sons and daughters that will create unity like never before. His honour and His glory will prevail. The least of these will be lifted up and positioned to create a syncopation with all of heaven. When this happens, we will see the fruit of healings, deliverance, and salvation.

I believe that God is awakening His Bride. He is calling forth ones that will be gathering together as an ecclesia within regions and areas; an ecclesia gathered in oneness through the heart of the Father. They will desire His heart for heaven to invade earth. They will see from heaven's perspective by ascending the ladder of His presence into heaven and then descending back down with the blueprints of His heart. This, in turn, will begin to affect the different mountains of influence in their regions. Thus, His Kingdom come, His will be done (Matthew 6:10 TPT).

Intercession through Heaven's Perspectives

God is calling the intercessors to a deeper level of intercession that is aligned with heaven's protocol in the Courts. This heavenly perspective will impact mindsets that will endure and not be shaken. The scripture states (Matthew 16:18), *"on this rock, I will build My church and the gates of Hades will not prevail."* When Jesus spoke these words, He did this in reference to Peter, the apostle; however, God is now building His church (ecclesia). This reformation within the church is not for self-gain but to bring His Kingdom here into the earthly realms and to see the sons of God come to maturity. Hence, our intercession is now being done from a Heavenly perspective as opposed to an earthy perspective. Our intercession is, therefore, more strategic and intentional.

New Sounds Emerging

Sounds from heaven in worship are coming that will burst forth God's love and healing like never seen before. Out of a place of resting in who we are, these sounds will be released. This will be straight from the Father's heart to the lost, wounded, and broken. These sounds will cause many to be creative and be slingshot into their destinies. Many will have heavenly downloads that will bring new inventions and solutions to earthly problems. It will be pure and will have an amazing effect in the atmosphere of regions and nations.

It will open up portals and doors into dimensions. Many will be restored and renewed to reign from a Kingdom perspective, which will attract more angelic activity. This will cause many to search their hearts and return to their first love, GOD. God says, *"Come up higher and go deeper into your relationship with Him."* Remember not to despise the days of small beginnings, for it will only take a small pebble to generate a ripple effect of a tsunami of His Love.

Carriers of a Dream/Ministry

I had a dream where I saw myself in a place where people were busy doing life. I saw my stepmother, and she told me she was pregnant again. She was trying her best to abort the baby because she could not afford to keep it. I encouraged her to carry the child to full term, and I would take the child and raise it.

I believe God is saying that there are ones who have carried a baby (ministry/dream) for some time, and they are getting weary and are trying to abort their baby (ministry/dream). God wants them to know that they have an inheritance that He has predestined for them, that if they birth that baby, He will make provision for them in all they do.

Restoration of the Prodigals

In an encounter, I saw various individuals. I knew one who was a believer many years ago but had fallen away from the ways of God. This male believer tried to speak to me, but he could not get the words out. Jesus placed His hand on his lips, and miraculously, he could speak without stuttering. I saw Jesus' smile, and He said, *"he will speak again as he did before."* I believe this word is for those who have prayed for loved ones who have fallen away from God. He is calling the prodigals to come home.

I am sensing God is going to restore and call the prodigals home to Himself (Luke 15:11-32). I believe restoration and healing are coming. God is rewriting and realigning people's destinies. Those who are in bondage will be free to run as they have been destined. I believe God is encouraging us to take heart that He will answer our prayers. Keep praying, and He will restore hearts to first love, and they too will be a part of reaping the great harvest that God is about release.

REFLECTIONS

Day 29

- Meditate on 17:28 *"in Him I live and move and have my being."*
- Allow the reality of what that means for your identity as a son of YHWH.
- Allow YHWH to activate and access your dreams.
- Let Him tutor you.

Day 30
True Love

By Marsha Brethour

His Ways Not Mine

I was awakened this morning with many questions in my head. I realized that the more I learn of YHWH in my journey with Him, the less I really know. There are so many things that do not make sense to me in my way of thinking. But if I let go of my own precepts and expectations, then YHWH is able to show me how He thinks. His ways are then made manifest, which reveals the very nature of who He is. It is likened to a painting made up of beautiful colors, lines, and depth. What starts out on a blank canvas, to the onlooker, seems at first to be just lines, which later becomes what the artist envisions.

The artist's hand is used to inspire and shape a true expression of creativity beyond what one could imagine. It is then we realized that our expectations and perceptions are no longer important. This beautiful creation is now revealed to be a masterpiece from YHWH. This is what our journey with YHWH should be; it allows the artist (YHWH) to make us into beautiful masterpieces for all the world to see.

The purpose is that others may be provoked into a deep longing for YHWH, which fuels us to pursue the One Who had pursued us from before we were born. In our deep pursuit of YHWH, we are then changed to become true sons, hence becoming the co-heirs YHWH created us to be to walk alongside Him. In our individual journey with Him, as sons and priests, we are called to mature into Kingship into upward perfection in Him. I am humbled by the knowledge that YHWH is good, mysterious, and marvelous in all His ways.

True Love

This brings me to the questions of *"Who is YHWH?"* and *"What is He?"* In one word, Love is who He is and what He is. Love is as defined in the Bible in 1 Corinthians 13: 1-13 MSG –

Verses 3-7
Love never gives up.
Love cares more for others than for self.
Love doesn't want what it doesn't have.
Love doesn't strut,
Doesn't have a swelled head,
Doesn't force itself on others,
Isn't always "me first,"
Doesn't fly off the handle,
Doesn't keep score of the sins of others,
Doesn't revel when others grovel,
Takes pleasure in the flowering of truth,
Puts up with anything,
Trusts God always,
Always looks for the best,
Never looks back,
But keeps going to the end.

Love is the very nature of YHWH. So, if we are to be like Him in our nature, should we not be love itself to those around us? Jesus is our blueprint to follow as we journey and co-labor through this earthly realm.

How can we say we love YHWH when we seem not to be able to simply love the ones we are in relationship with, like our families and extended communities (John 13:34-35; 15:11-15; 1 John 4:11-12 MSG)? We must first learn to love our enemies as ourselves and the ones who are different from us. Because even though we disagree, we can still love each other. Seeing each one as YHWH see us through the eyes of the Father in the Spirit because if we do not, we are just deceiving ourselves. Remember, we are called to be a royal priesthood, a peculiar people, a chosen generation (1 Peter 2:9-10 MSG). Also, be careful that you do not become a hindrance or a stumbling block to another person's journey with YHWH. When you are called to be a son, you are accountable for all you do and say to YHWH. Love is not a weakness, but true strength in YHWH. We are called to be love; Love already died for us. Now we have to die daily to ourselves so that we can be love to others all around us.

The more we love, the more we will become love Himself; as we do this, we will be able to transition, function, and be transformed into the fullness of true matured sons. Only then can we govern and reign and really bring heaven into the earthly realm.

REFLECTIONS

Day 30

- Meditate on 1 Corinthians 13:1-13
- Reflect on YHWH as LOVE.
- Who is YHWH to you?
- How am I accountable to Him as His son?

Day 31
Words Of The Father To Us

By Marsha Brethour

The Gift of God's Love

For God so [greatly] loved and dearly prized the world, that He [even] gave His [One and] [a]only begotten Son, so that whoever believes and trusts in Him [as Savior] shall not perish but have eternal life. (John 3:16 AMP)

I was awakened by Father with a reminder of His love and care for us as His children. He reminded me that I did not choose my family, but He did. As we go about our busy lives during the holidays, we sometimes forget about the real reason for the season. It is the fact that God sent His son to die for all of us so that we may all live. Living means being good stewards of what God has given to us, especially our families, the unsaved, saved, and unlovable ones. Father sent His Son to die for all. Therefore, as sons who are made in His likeness, we are all called to do the same towards our families, friends, colleagues, and acquaintances. With love, we will be able to see each person as Father sees them. Love is God's gift to His sons to show who He is to a loveless world.

Relationship, Restoration and Miracles

Many are facing adversities within their families, and they do not know what to do. I hear the Father saying, *"Just love and enjoy the people whom I have placed in your lives. You cannot change anyone, only I can."* says the Holy Spirit. *"Restoration and miracles are coming."* You will see through the Father's eyes, which will bring victory into marriages and families with unsaved loved ones. Relationship is God's priority, as we will see in this concept spilling out to our ecclesia, hubs, churches, and communities. Fostering our relationship with others will birth much fruit to the kingdom.

Tend the Garden of your hearts

I heard the Father say, *"tend to your gardens in heaven and see if there are any weeds that need to be rooted up so that advancement will take place quickly. As you root out these weeds, you will see from heaven's perspective, which will produce new growth and much fruit to appear in your lives. You will be able to legislate from a place of rest and joy. Engage with heaven and ask for the seven spirits of God to assist you in fulfilling your scrolls"* (Isaiah 11:2-3 AMP). Pure hearts, humility, and love will be our pathway towards gaining momentum in the heavenly realms.

Message to the Intercessors

Father says,

"don't be weary or discouraged but take courage. I have seen your tears, and I will bring forth victory to you. You have been faithful; I will cause your feet to be as hind's feet to jump over all hurdles. What I have started, I will complete. My promises will come to pass. Fix your eyes and position your hearts in a place of expectancy, and you will reap the fullness of My Spirit. Rest in Me, and I will show hidden, ancient pathways in the heavenlies. These pathways will lead you to the depths of My heart that few have accessed. Forget the old and move forward to what is ahead. How it may seem is not what it truly is. I am coming in a new fresh way. I am raising up communities of like-minded people who function from heaven's perspective. Each of your teardrops is encoded with My DNA, and it speaks and carries a frequency that breaks chains in the earth. Keep advancing, for I am with you."

Shalom.

REFLECTIONS

Day 31

Sit quietly and pray –
- *"Father, please walk with me in the garden of my heart."*
- Look to see what He is showing you.
- Dialogue with Yeshua about what is planted in your garden.
- Embrace relationship and community by seeing others through love.
- Fix your eyes on the Being of Love – Yeshua. Become what you behold

About The Authors

Marsha Brethour is a son/forerunner, seer, prophetic worshiper, blogger, former educator, florist, wife and mother to five children. Kadeem, Kris, Michael, Andrew and Rosie. She has been in service in various capacities within the church from lay minister, prophetic intercessor to worship leader and has walked with YHWH since the age of thirteen.

Marsha has served as lay minister, prayer and prophetic intercessor and choir member at CCCOG in Florida for six years then moved to Canada to serve at MCA as a choir member and intercessor. She also served at Catch Fire Ministries (CTF) Scarborough on the worship and prophetic team for seven years. After marrying Dale in 2013, they served at Family Worship Center Uxbridge as worship leaders.

Dale Brethour, Marsha's husband, is the co-author of this book. He is a son, Apostolic Elder at Family Worship Center, worship leader, song writer, trucker, husband and father. Dale has been a pioneer within his sphere of influence yet hidden away for many years. YHWH has used him various ways to touch the lives of many through worship, leadership and cross pollination within the Body of Christ. His hunger for more intimacy with YHWH has brought him into this new global move.

Both Dale and Marsha have been affiliated with Ecclesia of Burning Ones (EBO) and were members of Walking Off the Map and more recently, Ignite Hubs Canada. Marsha and Dale are willing vessels who have embraced riding the wave of YHWH's heart to facilitate the process of seeing the sons arise in true maturity and perfection for the glory of YHWH in the age of enlightenment.

They love the Body of Christ and their hearts is to see all come to the fulfilment of their destinies the way YHWH intended.

Citations

Quantum Glory by Phil Mason.
Re-ordering your day by Chuck Pierce for various excerpts on
Hebrew words.
Research via internet searches on the Greek word.
Prophetic interpretations from Robin Dhillon (friend) and Dale
Brethour (co-author)

www.ingramcontent.com/pod-product-compliance
Lightning Source LLC
Chambersburg PA
CBHW072108090426
42739CB00012B/2884